PICTURES IN THE WINDOW

A REFLECTION ON THE LIFE OF THE ARTIST
WILLIE DORAN

DEIRDRE DEVINE

PIER
PUBLICATIONS

First Published in Ireland
by Pier Publications 2001

ISBN Number : 0-9539486-0-9

Printed by: Nicholson & Bass

Typesetting, Layout & Cover Design: John Quigley

Photography : Paul Kavanagh
Additional photographs supplied by Madaleine Cleuth, Stella Devine,
Daniel Doherty, Susan Doran and John McGrory

Assisted By
Donegal County Council
Deontas Mhic an tSaoir Award 2000

FOR MY PARENTS
JOHN JOE AND DEIRDRE MC GRORY

ACKNOWLEDGEMENTS

This story has been written with the help of many people who shared with me their memories of Willie Doran. Its illustration was made possible by the generosity of those who allowed works by the artist, in their possession, to be reproduced. I thank them all for their assistance and cooperation.

I am grateful to Dr. Nicola Gordon Bowe for kindly writing such a fine introduction. Appreciation must be given to John Quigley for his excellent work on the cover design and layout of text and illustrations. Sincere thanks to Paul Kavanagh for photographing a collection of the artist's work. Acknowledgement is also due to Madaleine Cleuth, Stella Devine, Daniel Doherty, Susan Doran and John Mc Grory for providing additional photographs.

To members of the Doran family, Madaleine Cleuth, Veronica Reddington (nee Doran), Susan Doran, Teddy & Nan Doran, George Doran, Veronica McGuigan, Sadie O Kane, Eileen McGeady and to the late Joe Doran, I express my appreciation. To my father, brothers, sisters and friends, who were instrumental in encouraging this tribute, I acknowledge my gratitude. Special thanks must be given to my husband, Vincent and to Ciaran, Stephen and Louise, without whose ongoing patience and support this work could not have been completed.

In conclusion, I gratefully acknowledge the following for their contribution: Roy Anderson, Elizabeth Balmer, Lady Pamela Blunden, Rev.B.Colton, Brendan & Gertie Bonner, Cartha Byrne, Conall Byrne, Tom & Mae Byrne, Dr. David Caron, John & Briget Connolly, Edward & Caroline Crumlish, The Devine Family, Dr. Joseph & Ann Enright, Sean & Teresa Farren, Joan Faulkner, the late Brendan Faulkner, Frank Galligan, Tom & Ann Grace, Ann Harris, Ross Harvey, Rev. J. Irwin, the Lynch family, Paddy Kelly, Rev. P. McArdle S.J., Paddy McCrossan, Peter McKenzie, Angela McLaughlin, Carrie McLaughlin, David McLaughlin, Martin & Bridie McLaughlin, Kathleen McLaughlin, Margaret & Michael McLaughlin, Cornelius & Philomena McFeely, McGrory's, Culdaff, the Mills family, the O Connor family, Brigid O Donnell, Kathleen Ruddy, Oliver & Monica Simpson, Tim Stampton, John & Elaine Quigley, Irene Vail.

Contents

BLACK AND WHITE ILLUSTRATIONS

All work illustrated is by Willie Doran

LIST OF COLOUR PLATES

INTRODUCTION
'The World in a Grain of Sand'

On my first extended visit to Donegal, I can remember clearly lying, face-down on the strand at Magheramore, and being overwhelmed by the incredible intricacy and wonder of each tiny shell which went to make up what had at first appeared to be sand on the beach. That each tiny shell would be ground down in time to form such a huge immeasurable expanse, having had its clear identifiable form, was both comforting and daunting. But for this book, Willie Doran might just have been another small star in a huge galaxy, a well-respected memory, whose unique skills, experience and appearance would have gradually faded into the fabric of Culdaff's history. Deirdre Devine has ensured that this will not happen.

With careful respect and an artist's eye for the details and usages of his life and the village and landscape that surrounded him, she has recorded with affection and perception the passage of one consistently committed, gifted life in a quiet Donegal village. By writing down her memories and observations, as well as her many conversations with an admired friend and mentor, she has thereby also recorded a world of simple, natural pleasures and containment that is fast disappearing before our eyes. Particularly memorable in her account are Doran's proud respect for his immediate environment, which involved regular whitewashing of kerbs and walls, his neat, immaculate appearance, his careful (and ecological) self-sufficiency, his preference for "soft green and earthy shades" as he worked in his little kitchen filled with the glowing morning sun, his illusionistic painted surfaces, his precious horde of "private possessions of importance, gathered up over the years", housed with his art materials in a "small four-door cupboard", his bicycle trips to buy signwriting and painting materials in the market town of Carndonagh, or the 52 mile round ride to Derry, which became more occasional and by bus as he got older. Graphically, she records his grateful wonder at being "blessed with the gift of sight", his delight at the early morning peace as he travelled past the familiar landmarks of "the still under-populated countryside of his native Inishowen", before browsing and visiting the newly opened Orchard Gallery in the increasingly war-torn city. She introduces the painters he admired, unfamiliar names, and tells us how much he learned from his monthly magazine, *The Artist,* a constant source of information once he had had to discontinue his art studies in Dublin after four enchanted years.

Those four years of Willie Doran's all-too-short involvement with Sarah Purser's co-operative stained glass studio, an Túr Gloine, were how I became involved in this story, and it is thrilling for me to travel in time and see the photographs of the good-natured young man taken in 1937-8, during the four years of his stained glass study and work in Dublin. We see Doran laughing with the glazier Charlie Williams in the garden of the studio in Pembroke Street, see him cuddling Catherine O'Brien's cat, posing with O'Brien and Williams or on the steps of Mespil House, the large eighteenth century canal-side house which his patron, the distinguished painter Sarah Purser made her headquarters in Dublin. Aged 88, as she had done to other burgeoning artists during her long life, she extended her esteemed and confident protection to the 24 year old, offering the un-dreamt-of possibility of night classes at the National College of Art, the first and only formal training he ever had. She also gave him the unique experience of working alongside artists of the calibre of Michael Healy and Evie Hone, both at the peaks of their respective careers in stained glass, and each deeply respectful of each others spiritual and artistic gifts. Healy, a lifelong member of the studio would be unexpectedly dead by 1941, while Hone, who converted to Roman Catholicism in 1937, having finally persuaded Purser to admit her as a full member of the studio in 1935, was learning to translate her paintings into deeply glowing windows. It can only be our loss that the Emergency came so soon, leading to the closure of the studio and any possibility of a career for Doran in such a demanding craft. I look forward to seeing the names of firms that Devine tells us he painted on glass windows, as well as on delivery vans, on decorative signs and on shop fronts, since the artistic incorporation of lettering into an overall design was always insisted upon by Sarah Purser. It was also one of the identifying factors in each village and town. I also look forward to reading Doran's reminiscences of An Túr and Mespil House, and to seeing more of his portable and mural artwork, including the miniature turf houses and farmyards he made for a time. The quiet satisfaction and skill he brought to the undemonstrative but no less professional painterly trade techniques perfected over a lifetime were once valued by communities all over Ireland and beyond. Such qualities deserve recognition as much as the fine stained glass windows whose production in an unimposing Dublin workshop was to inspire him in 1962 to return as a painter to his native peninsula.

Nicola Gordon Bowe (Dr.)
March 2001
Art and Design historian.
Writer and lecturer in the History of Art and Design
at the National College of Art and Design, Dublin.

PREFACE

My mother often used the phrase "I could write a book…" when she was recounting a memorable tale. *Pictures in the Window* is a story based on the memorable life of an artist whose talent and dedication to his work gained the respect of all who knew him.

We had the good fortune in Culdaff to have someone like Willie Doran living among us. I was further privileged in that he played an important role in our family home when we were growing up. My parents were keen patrons of his work and involved him in the decoration of their hotel for over fifteen years. He was a friend and mentor during my early days as an art student and an inspiration to all who paint the magical landscape of Inishowen.

Pictures in the Window is a personal tribute to an artist who, in his day, produced an exceptional body of work. Willie's capabilities were noteworthy and varied but only a relatively small audience accessed the range of his achievements during his lifetime. I hope that through my recollections, many more people will come to enjoy the great talent and personality that was Willie Doran.

Deirdre Devine
March 2001

1. Culdaff Village, Winter
1977
Watercolour

Chapter One
A Morning to Remember

December sunlight danced against the kitchen window. Willie Doran sat at the table looking down the Forge Brae while he ate his breakfast. There was little movement at that time of a Sunday morning in Culdaff. Most people would be waiting to get up for the second Mass at eleven o' clock. He always went to the earlier one at half past eight, as that left a better quality of day ahead and there were often things to be done.

It was unusually bright for the time of year, Willie thought, as he ate a slice of toast and wiped some marmalade which had accidentally found its way onto his thumb. He disliked the feeling of anything sticky on his hands, being by nature a very particular person. Only a few days before, he had remarked that fact to a young neighbour, who often called in to his house since taking up the study of painting. Over the past five years, she had visited him on numerous occasions, to discuss aspects of her own work and of his. The 'Maestro' was the name by which her father fondly and appropriately referred to Willie Doran, for he was well known locally as a gifted artist.

Enjoying company from time to time, he took a keen interest in the progress of the young painter. She delighted in seeing his work at various stages of completion and he had begun, recently, to share with her, some of the joys and frustrations of what is essentially, a solitary occupation. Her inspiration to study art had been derived from watching him at work. There were many times, as a child, when she had the opportunity to do that. Growing up with a number of his paintings on the walls of her family's home, she was well aware of his talent from an early age. Yet the young woman, like many of her neighbours, had accepted it as commonplace, for years in the tiny locality, to have among them a person of exceptional gifts and only began to fully appreciate his greatness as she matured.

The artist lived and worked in a small, terraced house in the County Donegal village. An end dwelling in a row of four, it stood at one of the best vantage points on the height, facing down towards a broad, single street. O'Connors, next door, enjoy the clearest and most complete view, but Willie's kitchen window opened onto the winding road and with the church tower, trees and two neatly facing rows of houses and shops before him, it also had an enviable scene to behold. He was well situated for observing the unfolding lives of the people who lived there.

The house was noticeable, in those days, for its decoration of brightly coloured brickwork. He had painted the exterior walls with a suggestion of pale yellow, brown and green rectangles, subtly delineated into neat rows and with clever light and shadow effects, imitating the type of facing blocks which were fashionable in modern buildings during the Sixties and Seventies. Many business premises, as well as some private houses in Culdaff and other nearby towns, sported a similar appearance on their walls at that time. Because of his ingenious ability to suggest, with paint, numerous variations of natural stone, Willie had received many commissions to create this effect locally. His own home was exceptional, as he had been able to experiment freely with colour and shape there and explored daring combinations not possible with a brief from other patrons. It made a striking feature to behold on the corner, when passing through the village.

Born on the fifth of June 1912, he had been named William Bernard Doran. His mother, Kathleen, was one of the Mc Laughlins from Culdaff. She married Joseph Doran, whose family originated from County Wexford and they had five children. Willie was the eldest and the others were Kathleen, Mary Bernadette, known as Mollie, Joseph and Veronica. His childhood was spent in Culdaff and from an early age he showed remarkable artistic ability.

When he was a young man of twenty four, Willie received a unique opportunity to develop his talent. He studied art in Dublin, under the guidance of Miss Sarah Purser, the distinguished portrait painter and founder of An Túr Gloine, a co-operative stained glass enterprise. The prestigious co-operative included among its members at that time, artists such as Michael Healy and Evie Hone, whose creations, in buildings throughout Ireland and abroad, continue to testify to their genius. Through Miss Purser's sponsorship, Willie had the privilege of working in the acclaimed studios between the years 1936 and 1940.

On returning to Culdaff, he had stayed at home until 1948, when he left again to spend fourteen years in England. There, in the town of Crewe, he trained in sign writing and interior decorating. Thus was established an ability, not only as an artist but also as a very competent sign painter and decorator of buildings, inside and out. Coming home finally in 1962, he had settled in the village, remaining there since then and earning a living from his artistic skills.

He made a comfortable living by modest standards. It was enough to do a single man, he always assured himself. By the late years of the Seventies, his reputation was well established in that part of Donegal and beyond. People came to his home regularly to commission paintings, especially of the beautiful landscape to be found in the surrounding peninsula of Inishowen. He had just finished an oil painting. It was a commissioned piece and depicted a view of the pier at Malin Head, Ireland's most northerly point, which is about twelve miles from where he lived.

Willie sighed. Nearly all his work in the past two decades had been to order. An accomplished landscape painter, he was always in demand. So much was the demand, in fact, that he had found himself wishing lately to have a little more time to experiment with certain subjects, simply for his own pleasure. A picture form-ing in his mind had begun to haunt him. It was a scene, full of birds, crows or seagulls, packed so tightly together in flight that the sky almost completely disappeared behind their forms. It would be a challenge to a looser, more daring approach, which he was striving to develop in his painting in recent years.

Although he had a growing desire to commit his personal visions to paint, Willie Doran's patrons always came first. An artist, whose living had, for years, depended on the commissions of various types he received, their needs must be observed.

"Work is work," he reminded himself. "Someday I'll paint that picture." The promise was made silently as he sat, leisurely sipping a hot cup of tea and gazing at the familiar scene which curved peacefully before him.

Culdaff is a small, planned type of village. Straddling the low hill, on which rests a once thriving blacksmith's forge, its central focus is a triangular shaped green, flanked on each side by roads. The main road leads to Moville or Malin, depending on the direction from which a traveller approaches. A short, link road passes the row of houses where the artist's home stood and a third leads through the village to the shore, which is approximately a mile away.

An old pump, that once used to provide the inhabitants with water, stands gracefully idle in its shelter on the green. Looking slightly faded and dilapidated in those days, the shelter, or pump house, comprises a pyramid shaped canopy roof on four slender uprights. Though in bad need of a coat of paint at that time, it was still noticeable for its elegance. A gift to the people of Culdaff in 1908, from the Young family who lived on the large estate outside the village, it commemorated the Golden Jubilee of Mr and Mrs Young. Since the decline in need for a central supply of water, it had become disused. Now it was simply a favourite play spot for children. A few months earlier, Willie had produced a small but beautiful watercolour of the ageing pump in its shelter, contrasting the faded, pink painted woodwork with the lush grass of the surrounding green and a tree in full summer blossom. He had captured, in the tiny painting, something of the stately character of an impressive feature, having often admired its enduring grace from his kitchen window.

Situated on the northeastern coastline of Inishowen, Culdaff has for many years been a popular holiday destination. The White Shore nearby, is a safe and attractive beach with four strands, where the sand is not white but beautifully golden in colour and the Atlantic Ocean washes against low, grey rocks and the distinctively rising headland of Dunmore. Visitors from Europe, America and parts of the British Isles have long been drawn to the area.

The river there is noted for good fishing and was always a hive of activity throughout the summer. Two bridges give access to the village, as it winds lazily to the estuary at the bay. Below one of the bridges is a strange, boat shaped stone, known locally as St Buadan's Boat. It was believed that St Buadan, the patron saint of the area, left the mark of his own fingers in the stone. Tradition states that the saint, on being pursued in Scotland, escaped miraculously. The edge of the cliff, on which he stood, dropped into the sea and he was transported, on the rock, to the Inishowen port and from there to a place upstream where it still remains.

Devotion to St Buadan had always been strong in the parish. A well, associated with him, could be found at the other side of the bridge, behind the graveyard of the small church bearing his name, which stands in the centre of the village. The well had been noted for cures down through the centuries and people once made a turas, or pilgrimage there, invoking the help of the saint in their daily lives. The tradition had largely died out in the present century, although Willie remembered a time when his mother's sister, Fannie Mc Laughlin, professed a strong faith in St Buadan. She made a turas annually throughout her lifetime and was probably the last regular pilgrim in the parish, up to her death in 1969.

Bunagee is the name of the harbour and was another favoured spot for fishing. Throughout the season, a few folk could nearly always be found standing at the edge of the pier, gazing intently out into the sea. Occasionally, their lines would be tautly stretched in the lively promise of a catch. More often they waited, hour after hour, for a fish to bite, somewhere in the nearby coastal depths of the Atlantic. He admired those patient fishermen and enjoyed, at times, standing on the pier beside them, silently watching their lone crusade, as they faced the vastness of the wide ocean, teeming below its surface with an abundance of life.

A few boats were kept at Bunagee, along with a trawler or two owned by men from Culdaff or from the Glengad area nearby. The estuary, known locally as the Mouth of the River, was always rich in sand eels. Watching two men there once, knee deep in water and engrossed in the task of eel gathering, Willie had painted the scene in his youth. He depicted wiry men, with shirt sleeves rolled up and trousers pulled high to reveal bare legs, as they bent over, crouched low and reached into the water to trap their slippery game. An intensity in their concentration and the peacefulness of the setting had inspired the fine, large watercolour which now hung on the kitchen wall, reminding him of former times and youthful, lazy summers.

The tourists were long gone that morning and the empty street echoed only with the quiet sounds of winter. Somewhere a dog barked. Cattle moaned in a distant byre. A cat mewed softly as it slipped down past his window. Hens and roosters could be faintly heard, clucking and crowing, heralding the beginning of another day. Suddenly a flock of dark crows rose from their large, apparent nests, in the vacant trees around the grey church tower, causing the sky to fill for a few moments with their rowdy movement. The startling motion held his attention briefly. Later the bell would sound, filling the air also with its low, distinctive tones, as it summoned a congregation to morning service in the little church.

Willie turned from the window to look at his painting. The satisfaction of having completed a successful picture made him smile. He thought he would ask his young friend to come and have a look at it later, if he saw her in the street. She often walked down past his window. She would usually see him there if she went by early in the morning. He would jokingly wave a slice of toast or hold up a cup of tea to cheer her on her journey. He would raise his head from reading the paper and smile broadly as other neighbours hurried by. People glanced in as they passed. It was customary to salute a familiar presence. Sometimes Willie could be found at the window, deep in concentration as he worked on a painting. Frequently, he would be there, just as he was that day, sitting contentedly, his eyes fixed on the street, while he looked with expectant interest at the quiet scene before him.

Sunlight flickered through the branches of a tree on the green. It was a fine, round shaped tree and a subject which had inspired many spontaneous sketches, as well as being included in some of his larger paintings over the years. He had studied it in summer, when its deep, green foliage shaded a corner of the house. Observing the changing colour in autumn to a rusty orange, he had painted it again, clothed in glorious, golden hues. With leaves shed, its raw form had been explored finally in the depths of winter, as the empty branches stretched before him, silent against a dramatic array of clouds.

Working often, during the past year, in a small sketch book which was always kept to hand, numerous studies of the village green had been made. Maintaining the practice of regularly drawing from observation, throughout his lifetime, spare hours were filled working from the front window. This offered a range of viewpoints of the various pictorial elements that could be found within the confines of the street. Painting the words 'NO PARKING', on the edge of the road outside his home, ensured that the view was never interrupted. Using a variety of media, lively and delicate observations had been produced. Willie had chuckled to himself one day, as he rapidly sketched some workers with the Donegal County Council, who were carrying out road mending on the Forge Brae, two or three months previously. Noting the activity, he had captured their labouring movements with a few deft strokes of his pen. When they stopped for tea, a quick sketch was made of the spades and shovels that had been left resting idly against the wall. Employing the unique wit and instinctive sense of humour that was a special feature of the Doran style, the drawings were labelled individually. The first he entitled *Council men working,* while the second became *Council men not working!* Enjoying a joke, humour was naturally incorporated into aspects of his art, even in the privacy of a sketchbook.

That morning the trees were stark, but were warming slowly in the sun, which lit the whitewashed walls, in front of the old graveyard opposite, with a soft glow. Willie often wondered about the people who had lived here, years before and who now lay, eternally sleeping, close to his home, under the increasing roar of traffic and the light-hearted sounds of children playing. Some of the original graves had been below where the road was built. Others could be discovered by picking carefully through the tall weeds and undergrowth behind the nearby wall. There was a black, iron gate leading into the graveyard and a few inscribed slabs showed the trades and identities of people who had once dwelt and worked in the area. Dating back over a couple of centuries, names and symbols told part of the early history of Inishowen.

There must have been skilled tradesmen here in their day, he often reflected, looking up towards the Roundstone, a low circular wall, enclosing a neat flower bed and a maturing tree, which sat out from the larger wall surrounding the ancient graveyard. Much of our local heritage, he supposed, was now enshrined behind its whitewashed facade. Willie Doran had a great respect for tradesmen, having a modest satisfaction in being skilled in his own field of practice. He was noted, by all who knew him, for taking as much care over the papering of a wall or the mixing of a colour to paint a room, as he did in the creation of a masterly piece of landscape painting or a finely executed portrait. The day of the multi-skilled tradesman was coming to an end, he feared, as new ways were replacing old with increasing rapidity.

A lone dog wandered idly down the street. In search of food, it sniffed casually at anything of interest.

"Haven't dogs the great times of it?" he thought. "That boy hasn't a care in the world!" The comment was stated aloud as the unconcerned creature carried on nosily down the road, oblivious to the fact that anyone was watching.

"I wonder where he's heading?" the questions continued, as the purpose of the journey began to take on a curious fascination, if only for a fleeting moment. "Isn't he glad to be getting a bit of peace in the street, with nobody about to bother him at this time of the day?"

Appreciating the early silence himself, Willie followed the animal's frolics as it made its way along the deserted village. Finishing the last drop of tea in his cup, he strained to catch the final stages of its progress. The dog sniffed on, regardless that it had become another element of focus for a quiet observer's thoughts that day. He watched it weaving in and out, through the grass and down the hill, until it reached a gap between two houses and disappeared out of his view.

The street resumed its earlier solitude. Apart from the quiet ramblings of other occasional creatures and the ever increasing calls of the birds, no one else had stirred. The scene was there for his pleasure, uninterrupted on that bright Sunday morning, at least for the moment.

2. Council men, not working
1979
Pen and Ink

3. Council men, working
1979
Pen and Ink

4. The Pump, Culdaff Village Green
1979
Watercolour

Like many bachelors before him the Inishowen artist had spent years becoming self-sufficient. His house was immaculate inside and out and was always maintained to perfection. Willie took a great pride in its upkeep and also in the upkeep of the entire village green. He regularly whitewashed its low kerbs and the walls of the Roundstone close by. On entering his home, or even on giving a casual glance in while walking past, a fine mural could be seen on the interior wall of the hallway. Depicting an imaginative view of his own creation, the painting gave an impression of a large vertical window opening onto a wide vista. It suggested a feeling of space within the small area and was a colourful sight to encounter from the street.

The hallway led to the kitchen from the right and from the left a door opened onto the lower room of the house. Both had other rooms adjoining. The one from the lower side was the bedroom and a narrow scullery, as well as a room for storage, led from the kitchen. Willie looked around the little kitchen where he lived and worked. It was neat, compact and glowing in the morning sun, with the soft green and earthy shades for which he had a preference. He had papered the walls, some years before, with a delicately patterned wallpaper and the wooden surrounds and doors had been painted in carefully matching colours. Two bright yellow chairs, with speckled plastic covering, complemented the warm tones.

A sturdy, black range sat snugly in the chimney-breast which had been decorated, like the outside of the house, with the painted blocks effect. Carefully arranged in a variety of sizes and shapes, grey bricks, intersected with white lines, created the illusion of a neatly built, stone fireplace. A painting of a dark kettle, boiling merrily on an orange flamed fire, had been carried out on the back wall, behind the range top. Some ornaments from past days inhabited the shelf above, completing a homely scene. The warmth, with which the tidy room had been infused, was characteristic of an innate good taste and a well refined skill in the art of interior decorating. It also displayed Doran's active ingenuity which could create lively and humorous effects very easily with a few basic materials.

At the side of the range, beyond the turf box, a small, four-door cupboard housed all the necessities of an artist. Private possessions of importance, gathered up over the years, were stored in one section. Oil paints, charcoal sticks, watercolours; various media for mixing and a selection of varnishes were but some of the essential items stored in the other half. Access to that cupboard, as indeed access to the room off the kitchen, was not usual in the presence of a visitor. Willie enjoyed his privacy and maintained reserve when he considered it to be appropriate. A methodical man, every item was stored in careful order and supplies were updated with occasional journeys to Derry. At that time, the city was the nearest place where artists' materials could be bought and going there gave him a chance to further his knowledge about the ever increasing flow of new products coming onto the market. Sometimes he combined shopping trips with a visit to an exhibition, in one of the city's galleries. Although usually travelling alone, he had recently attended an interesting exhibition there, in the company of Paddy Mc Crossan, a painter from Carndonagh who was a keen admirer of Willie Doran's work.

A favoured artist of Willie himself was Arthur H. Twells. He frequently spoke of his admiration for this fine painter of landscape. He had first heard about the work of Twells while living in Crewe, having read an article about him in a publication of *The Artist* magazine. That was back in the 1950s, when Twells had received acclaim, for work produced while studying on one of the painting courses promoted through the magazine. A short article about the success of his one-man show, held in Derry, was featured in the English publication. The Northern Ireland based painter had exhibited a series of watercolours and had suddenly found himself in the limelight, among art lovers in the city and surrounding area. Willie remembered how heartwarming it had been then to read about the success of someone close to home, at a time when he was so far away himself. He continued to take an active interest in the work of Arthur Twells, on his return to Ireland in later years.

Always enjoying the opportunity of visiting galleries and exhibitions, he had done so when living both in England and in Dublin previously. As a student in Dublin, during the 1930s, Willie was able, for the first time, to frequent exhibitions of national and international importance. Seeing high quality, original works of art, sometimes in the freshness of their recent execution, was an experience which he cherished and which was retained within memory, to constantly enrich his understanding of his own painting practice. The informative monthly publication, to which he had subscribed regularly while in Crewe, had also kept him abreast of current developments. Thus he maintained a lively pursuit of and interest in the fine arts of painting and sculpture, throughout his mature life, even while serving his time as a sign writer and decorator.

The Artist magazine actually became an essential part of Willie's ongoing education, as a painter, when he was in England. It provided a platform for professionals, in Fine Art and Commercial Design areas, to show examples of their work and to pass on invaluable lessons to the reader. Subscribing to the publication for over ten years, many of his noted techniques and practices were developed from the inspiring examples he found there. Years later, he could still glean important information, on referring to the vast amount of copies which had been accumulated at that time. Keeping them close at hand, they were stored safely in his home, to assist with the generation of new ideas and to provide important background knowledge for further development of existing skills.

An avid reader, the Culdaff painter had always been intrigued by new innovations. Exhibitions of significance had been advertised and reviewed regularly in *The Artist*. Works by renowned British, European and American painters and sculptors were publicised there. Well-illustrated examples and colour copies of original work, to view in the comfort of one's own home, were available for continuous referral. This type of inspiration was invaluable when he was living in Crewe, as Willie had to further his knowledge of landscape and figure painting at that time, mainly through his own initiative and much self-development.

Working often from memory while in England, he produced a number of studies of scenes from home. More frequently, during those years, he was inspired by figurative subjects. Having studied the disciplines of drawing and painting in the National College of Art in Dublin, over a period of four years, an active interest was maintained in current practice taking place both in Ireland and beyond. While working by day as a sign writer and decorator in Crewe, Willie attended life drawing classes at night, to continue his studies, which had been left unfinished in 1940. This discipline, along with establishing a habit of regular sketching practice, paved the way for the accomplished paintings he would produce in later years, when he returned finally to Inishowen.

As monthly art publications were not available in Culdaff, full advantage was now taken of his occasional trips to Derry. While ensuring a visit to the more traditional type of gallery found in the city then, he also enjoyed the experience, recently, of calling into the Orchard gallery, which had just opened to promote visual work of a contemporary local and international nature. Interested in the new development, he was keen to observe the changing directions taking place. Sometimes an opinion was shared with his young friend from Culdaff, about exhibits they had both seen. They had enjoyed numerous discussions on a variety of works over the past few years. She treasured the confidence of the mature artist then in her own new found experience. Willie was reticent with comment when he did not like a piece of work. His silence often spoke more than his words, but he was gentle in his criticism of a beginner. In contrast, he enthused with pleasure, which was obvious from the glow on his face and from an excited tone in his voice, when he observed a well-handled effect in a painting. Having a keen eye for quality, he was a lover of naturalistic landscape painting and marvelled continuously at the accomplishments of artists such as Twells and his able contemporaries, who appeared to achieve such striking mastery of their techniques with a deceptive ease. A young student learned much about appreciating good painting from a conversation with Willie Doran in the kitchen of his house.

Having acquired a great deal of knowledge about the decorating trade over the years, as well as amassing a wealth of creative experience, his expert advice was readily sought by many people in the village and beyond. Problems related to painting and decorating, as well as those of an artistic nature, were regularly attended to when callers came to the door. For his sign writing, interior and exterior painting work, a range of products could be bought locally. Many items were available in Culdaff, or in the nearby market town of Carndonagh. Willie could cycle there easily on a dry day as it was only six miles away. Most of the materials he used were portable and could be transported, with a minimum of effort, on the carrier of a bike. If a job was extensive or required very bulky products, he usually travelled, with the person who had requested the work, to the most convenient supplier and the necessary goods would be taken back by car.

When his own artists' materials were needed, however, the jour-ney to Derry had to be made on the bus. It seemed only a short time ago when he would have travelled to Derry also on the bike. From Culdaff that meant a round trip of fifty-two miles. Willie enjoyed the run when he was a younger man. It was great being out in the air on a good day, but he wouldn't deny that sitting comfortably in the bus, recently, had its advantages.

A trip to Derry was always an adventure. Leaving home at eight-fifteen in the morning, he would board the Lough Swilly bus, which took a route through Gleneely, a neighbouring village about three miles away. He would travel on from there to Moville, for a further connection to Derry. The early morning journey brought him over the hill roads of Moneydarragh, before reaching Moville, a small town on the banks of Lough Foyle. There he would find a connecting bus which made its way beside the soft, water lapping shores of the wide lough, until it reached their final destination. The steeply rising form of Benevenagh, towering above the flat coastline of County Derry, could be viewed in the distance at the far side of the water, as they sped along the main road to the Border at Muff.

By 1979, the historic walled city had been unfortunately scarred by ten years of The Troubles. Willie reflected more and more, as he travelled there, how bleak Derry had become in recent years, behind tall, security fences and the constant uncertainty of impending violence. Explosions and the ensuing demolition that followed, had already taken their toll on many of the shops, hotels and other landmarks that were once familiar ports of call for people of his generation. Rebuilding would eventually restore its former glory, but in the years of the Seventies the outlook seemed bleak. Despite the gloomy state of parts of the city at that time, he was never deterred from the enjoyment he found in browsing in the artists' section of a good stationery shop in Shipquay Street. He continued also to take great pleasure from discovering many fascinating works displayed within the few galleries there, which maintained a strong promotion of the arts, in the face of all the destruction and strife that had so cruelly beset the northern province.

By far though, the most inspirational part of the day for him was the tranquil morning journey through the still under populated countryside of his native Inishowen. Often, at that hour, no other passengers would board the bus until after it had passed through Gleneely. Willie had time then to enjoy the silence of the country at its best and without interruption, could languish peacefully in the relative comfort of an enclosed viewing arena.

The road from Culdaff took him slowly uphill, past St Mary's Church at Bocan and on to the top of Birney Brae, a steep incline from where miles of the surrounding peninsula can be easily observed. It was marvellous, on a clear morning, to behold how much more of the landscape could be seen from the high vantage point of the bus, as it chugged its draughty way to their nearby destination. Green plains stretched out from Bocan towards Carndonagh in the distance. The large church there, with its imposing elevated position, could be seen, towering over the sprawling rooftops of the town which nestles in front of the gently rising mountain, Slieve Sneacht. Inishowen's highest peak, it was so named because it is always the first place to be covered with snow during the cold months of winter. It creates an impressive outline, higher than any other peak, within the range of hills visible when looking westward across the peninsula from Culdaff.

He would notice also, on the way, the ancient Stone Circle of Bocan, its remaining, tall, standing stones proudly and boldly braving the daily punishment of the elements. Aloft on a raised field they stand, often surrounded now only by a handful of hungry, grazing sheep. Testifying to the achievements of a people who had witnessed similar dawns there thousands of years before, he was continually reminded of the creativity that abounded in his own area in former times. The results of that creativity, he reflected, would probably continue to live on in the midst of all who pass, for many more centuries to come.

The bus would travel partly up the hill called Crucknanoneen. The view from its high summit, of the valleys below, was always spectacular. On a clear day, the outlines of Trawbreaga Bay, the hills of Glengad and the inlets of Culdaff and Tremone spread out behind a colourful patchwork of bog, field and roadways. From up there, houses seem like scattered pebbles on a garden of varied greenery, as the blue stripe of the Atlantic Ocean stretches gently along a wide horizon, only giving way, eventually, to a vast and ever changing sky.

Willie had made a number of journeys to Derry over the past few months, before the chill of winter set in. He knew that he had taken the trip more often recently than was usual. There had been materials to buy, but he was aware that he had been attracted to make the familiar journey this year, for reasons that were as much visually motivated as practically determined. Was it the enjoyment of the art exhibitions that drew him back, he wondered, or was it the glory of those mornings, travelling through a particularly beautiful part of the peninsula of Inishowen? Autumn shades had coated the hillsides since September and the purple hues of the late summer had relinquished their prominence, in October, to a luscious rust and ochre extravaganza. It was wonderful, he thought, to be blessed with the gift of sight and to be able to observe daily the constant changes of nature, which never fail to revitalise each season with nuances of colour and tone. The rich textures of the Irish landscape, in all the variations that the unpredictable weather reveals, could not be matched by anything else on earth.

Glancing around the kitchen, Willie's eyes took in the tidy order of the place. Resting his gaze, for a moment, on some of his own drawings and paintings which hung there, he noted how each one of them belonged to a slightly different stage of his development. Savouring the contents, of what he fondly considered to be his own private little gallery, he became gradually aware that the works displayed marked significant periods from his lifetime. They were small pieces in general. Some were framed and some were not. Yet they were all paintings and drawings with which he had been especially pleased at a time and he was proud to exhibit them in his home, firstly for his own pleasure but also for the perusal of any interested person who happened to call.

A youthful image was there. It was a delicate pen and ink draw-ing of Christ in Agony, which hung on the wall beside the kitchen door. Showing singular, early, competent though yet untrained draughtsmanship, a detailed mass of foliage surrounded the figure of Christ, kneeling, with hands clasped in anxious prayer, in the garden of Gethsemane. Willie knew its significance and the drawing had been framed in recognition of the important contribution it had made to his education as an artist. The skill and imagination, displayed in that work, had caught the attention of Sarah Purser and it was largely on the strength of the piece that she had offered training to him as a young man.

His eyes fell next upon the painting of the two sand eel gatherers at the Mouth of the River. A later work, it had been produced on his return to Culdaff in 1940. Here could be seen an educated observation of figures in tense activity, enhanced by his acquired mastery of technique and showing attention to the study of life, developed through hours of training in the College of Art. Combined with a fresh adventure into the medium of watercolour, creating bold tonal effects, it hung nearby. The glass protecting its delicate surface momentarily caught a ray of sunlight, that filtered through the curtains of the deeply set window, as Willie gazed at the long forgotten scene. Anxious then to apply his new skills to a local subject, he had been very pleased with that painting, which he always felt had retained its original vitality well, over the years.

A tiny oil study of the Long Strand at Culdaff Bay, with Dunmore Head in the background, hung on the wall opposite. It was painted in lively tones and depicted a blustery day on the nearby beach. A much later work, a palette knife had been used for this painting and a thick, impasto technique had been employed. It was a small piece, in comparison with some of his commissioned works, but showed a confident and assured command of his medium.

Produced some years before, by way of an experiment in the use of the palette knife, Willie had worked on the painting one day, after coming from the shore. A rapid piece, evoking the spirit of a place, he had achieved a very successful outcome. In the study, a freedom of handling, which he so often admired in other artists' work, had been accomplished in his own. It was executed some five years before, during a time when Doran was at the height of his productivity around the Inishowen area and also when he was very open to experimentation, in all aspects of his work. His interest in innovation extended naturally to his commissions. There, a traditional approach was generally sought, but for a painter, keenly aware of the need for constant development in his art, Willie experimented continuously, often producing interesting variations within the same recurring themes, which were requested time and again as subjects for paintings, especially of the local surroundings.

Close by, a melancholy, moonlit view, in the soft, finely applied oil brush technique of his most popular work, told the silent impression of another lone bicycle run to the shore in recent years. Again a small, spontaneous piece, it was painted in the recognisable style of the artist's late maturity. Depicting a full moon, shining high above the brooding form of Dunmore Head and reflected perfectly in the still waters of Culdaff Bay, it combined a subtle modulation of deep blue and grey tones. These were broken only by a glowing disc of pale silver and the delicate ribs of light which made the moon's reflection, in the gentle waves that lapped the silent shore.

Willie's eye strayed to the easel, which stood at the far side of the range, just beyond the centre of the floor. Strategically placed, to catch optimum light from a single bulb in the middle of the low ceiling above and the best of the daylight from the one, north facing window, it supported his large, recently commissioned painting, bringing a vibrant summer atmosphere to the little kitchen that morning. Displaying a delightful azure sky, with delicate, mauve tinged clouds floating just above the horizon, he had suggested the warm, indefinite line of distance, which is often seen far out on the sea during the months between June and August, when the weather is fine. The wildness of the Atlantic, at its most northerly in Ireland, had become gentle for a time, as a stretch of blue green sea calmed, to ripple eventually against the stony pier. A jagged outcrop of rock projected from the water in the middle distance. Some seagulls flew lightly, in front of a headland to the right of the picture, where a neat gathering of white cottages caught the sun, reflecting it wonderfully against a rich, mossy backdrop.

The easel would soon be empty again. The painting would be removed shortly and placed in the lower room to dry. It would only be brought out if someone with a special interest should call. Otherwise it would stay there until the buyer appeared for its collection. A black notebook would be checked to see which commission had to be undertaken next. Orders were carefully logged there and each was carried out as time and turn permitted. Willie Doran was unique as an artist, living and working in the area at the time. He was the only painter, in that part of Donegal, who made his living entirely from his skill in the visual arts and he was undoubtedly, by reputation far and near, the best. As such, there was always a backlog of patrons seeking his work. Having to cater for the many requests which were made of him as a sign writer and decorator also, the Inishowen artist had to manage his time carefully.

Reflecting back over the past two decades, he noted, with quiet satisfaction, how much of the locality had been enriched by the quality of his own handiwork. Evidence of lettering he had carried out could be seen along many of the roads, streets and on various buildings in the area. He had created decorative signs, advertising local hotels and other premises. Names of a variety of firms had been painted on glass windows and on the sides of their delivery vans, all requiring a high standard of clarity and often in demanding and complicated styles. Incorporating original colours and shapes, a sense of identity had been given to public houses, shops and restaurants. The skills Willie had learned, while serving his time in England, had edified Ireland's northern peninsula with an array of unique and stylish designs.

In recent times, the amount of commercial work undertaken by him had been reduced, particularly that of a large scale. Favouring instead, smaller, more manageable projects, a positive response was maintained to the numerous requests which came his way. Lately, he preferred to work as much as possible in the comfort of his home. It had become more conducive to his needs, in latter years, to work inside. Occasionally, however, it was still not unusual to find a delivery van parked on the street outside his house, while Willie expertly carried out a fine display of lettering on its side, working practically on the doorstep!

He continued also to paint a few signs. These were produced with great attention to a precise preparation in the measuring and drawing stage and incredible speed in the completion with a brush and paint, techniques which had been perfected over years of practice in the art of signwriting. More and more, in recent months, Willie was content to work on simple projects which brought a measure of personal satisfaction to himself and to complete as many of them as possible in the warmth of his own kitchen.

"There's no place like home," he smiled, looking fondly around his little studio.

5. Signwriting, Crewe 1950s

6. Christ in Agony
c1935
Pen and Ink

CHAPTER THREE
Important Influence

The formative years of a person are bound to have a lasting effect on how he approaches all aspects of later life. The early experiences of the gifted Culdaff man were no exception. Rising from the table, as the village awoke to an increasingly colder day, his mind turned constantly to incidents from the past. A sprightly figure for sixty-seven, Willie was dressed, as was usual once a week, in his Sunday best. That consisted of a white, smoothly ironed shirt with a tastefully matching tie. Dark trousers were belted firmly below his rather plump waist and on his feet he wore a pair of well polished, brown shoes. Noted locally for a pristine appearance, Willie always insisted on boiling white garments to ensure their sparkle. He faithfully undertook the labour of Monday hand washing, a task which many men of his day, living alone, might easily have neglected. A row of well scrubbed attire, airing on a wooden line in front of the kitchen range, was not an uncommon sight in his home.

The neatly groomed, outward features of the short, pleasant faced artist suggested the nature of the gentleman he was. Doran always dressed to suit the occasion. In winter he wore a long, grey overcoat and scarf for travelling outdoors, with a smart, peaked cap to shield his bare head. Now only a light coating of fine, snowy white locks remained there of the once thick, dark hair of his youth. In warmer weather, or for a casual outing, a short jacket and fresh, open necked shirt was worn. At the first hint of summer heat, he donned a sporting white T-shirt for easel painting and always protected his clothes with a serviceable pair of blue dungarees when decorating. A youthful outlook was reflected in his keen dress sense, which was enhanced by a ready smile and the warm twinkle in his eyes. Attention to a spruce appearance and his modest and friendly attitude made Willie Doran a welcome guest in any company.

Rolling up his sleeves, he began to wash the dishes. Some water was scooped from a bucket nearby to fill the kettle. He made a point of carrying the water daily from Jones' well, half a mile up the road, as he preferred the purity of its flavour to that of the village's piped supply. The painter was a familiar sight as he cycled back, often holding two teeming buckets expertly over the handlebars of the bike, while managing to steer easily around corners and down hills. The sheltered well, enclosed under a ceiling of sharp, hawthorn bushes, had been a welcome stop in his schooldays. Many a young traveller then, tired from a heavy bout of learning, would gladly cup his hands and partake of a refreshing drink from its clean, cold water on the long journey home. Brain-weary and hand-sore scholars looked for solace there, from the heat of prematurely sun drenched afternoons in the months of May or June, down through the years.

Schooldays, in the old building which once stood in the grounds of St Mary's chapel at Bocan, forged the beginning of an education that was to bring one Inishowen boy through many varied experiences, leading to his later development as an artist. There, along with the other children of the parish, Willie gained a basic introduction to reading, writing and arithmetic. Like all the youngsters of his day, he knew the joys and sorrows of a strict school training. He developed a well-styled handwriting, which stayed with him throughout his life, and a love of reading and history, as well as a great respect for the environment.

With most of the other children of his age, Doran left school early in his teens and sought work locally. The work to be found was of a practical nature and gave no indication of the future career which had been laid out for him. He assisted his father in an egg-sorting store for Faulkners of Culdaff. A natural ability for drawing, nevertheless, was to make itself felt early in his youth, as he often drew portraits of local characters, on the lime walls of his uncle Christy's home, with chalk. These were, for many years after, remarked upon by his contemporaries as being excellent likenesses and showed a facility for capturing the essence of a person in a few lines, a gift which he utilised to the full in later life.

The spirituality of his nature found expression in early pen and ink studies from imagination. Here he was able to combine a knowledge gleaned from close observation of his surroundings, animate and inanimate, with a growing interest in looking at reproductions of any works of art which were available at the time. Religious and secular work was studied carefully, in a desire to find out how various media could be used. Although he experimented readily and drew easily, Willie lived at a time when there was little opportunity for a young man, growing up in a rural environment, to further his capabilities in the field of artistic endeavour. Only those who had the financial means, whereby an education could be pursued, were at liberty then to follow the intentions of their hearts and acquire an artistic training. An occasional person, who showed special gifts, was sometimes the exception to the rule and in Willie Doran's case that is what happened.

The pen and ink study of Christ, which now hung in his kitchen, opened horizons for him, to an experience which was to colour his life and development from the age of twenty-four. The drawing was shown, with some other works, to Mrs Amy Young of Culdaff House. The Young family had been the land owners in the area for many years. Mrs Young had become aware of the creative talent of the aspiring local youth and his exceptional ability in drawing. She began to take steps to further his education.

Elsie, her sister, was married to John Purser, a nephew of the Dublin portrait painter. Through the influence of Mrs Young, Sarah Purser came to see the drawing. Impressed by the talent evident in a few pieces of work, the illustrious artist invited him to come to Dublin for training. Under her guidance and through her generous sponsorship, Willie was enabled to attend classes in the National College of Art, while working in the stained glass studios, An Túr Gloine, during the four years which preceded Miss Purser's retirement as director there.

It was a part of his life that he seldom spoke about and it seemed such a long time ago that morning. However, only a few days before, he had taken an unusual opportunity to talk briefly about the past to his young friend. She lived around the corner from him and worked a few nights of the week in her father's pub. He sometimes called in there for a drink. Willie would generally slip into the nearby pub for an hour or so, late in the evening, when there would already be a gathering of customers present. Making a point of never staying till closing time, he preferred to leave alone, long before the majority of other patrons would depart. Tiring early of his own company and the silence of a dark evening in winter, an unprecedented decision had been taken to go around for a drink that night at about eight o'clock. As it happened, she was in attendance behind the bar and because there was no one else in at the time, they were able to enjoy a pleasant and rather exceptional conversation. It had done the older man good to reminisce about past days and the discussion had ranged widely over many topics, reviving for him, at times unexpectedly, important and long hidden memories.

The young woman was interested to find out about Willie's early training. She was aware that he had studied with a painter of note in Dublin and because of the opportunity, presented by a quiet evening, she decided to question him tentatively about his past. Over the hours that followed, she was to learn, for the first time, about his years in Dublin and to hear also about his emigration to England. In the course of the night, he explained some of the unique developments which had taken place throughout his lifetime. Questions about working in stained glass provided an opportunity for him to speak about the studios called An Túr Gloine. Willie recalled Evie Hone, coming in to work, walking with the aid of a stick.

"She was lame," he said. Evie Hone suffered from a disability caused by infantile paralysis which caused her much physical hardship throughout her life.

"But she was gifted," he added, remembering some of the fine compositions he had seen her carry out in the studios, while he was there. He said that he had been pleased to work with another important figure in stained glass at the time, Michael Healy. Speaking enthusiastically about drawings produced by the artist, Willie had stated, with evident admiration,

"You should have seen the way Healy drew with pencil. I have never seen anyone, before or since, produce such beautiful work in line."

Doran was an admirer of good quality pencil drawing and his friend could sense the excitement with which the refined technique of the talented Dublin man was remembered and praised. As their conversation continued, he was reminded of some of the other people he had met. There was Miss O'Brien, with whom he was once photographed outside the studios and there was Charlie Williams, the skilled glazier from England, who had befriended him. Charlie was also photographed with Miss O' Brien and himself, at the back of the building that day in 1938. They had stood there in the sun, he recalled. Willie was holding a small cat in his arms. Was it Miss Purser's or one of Miss O' Brien's? Both had a fondness for the animals. Thinking back on those old prints reminded him vividly of his years with the famous co-operative.

He was young and anxious to absorb the many lessons that could be learned from the distinguished people who were its members. Miss Purser had provided him with a formal artistic training in drawing and painting, through enabling him to attend classes in the National College of Art, at night. He had also studied for a time in the Royal Hibernian Academy. He was taught by the respected artists and teachers of the day, including Sean Keating and Maurice Mc Gonigal. A daytime position had been found for him, by Sarah Purser, in the studios, where he assisted with a variety of activities taking place within the specialised craft and learned about the intricacies of painting on glass.

The young lady, anxious that night to find out about various aspects of his training, including the years he spent in England, had eagerly questioned him further. Willie obligingly told her about the apprenticeships he had completed while in Crewe, some years later. Surprisingly, he had enjoyed answering her questions, as she tried to piece together many hitherto unknown fragments of his life. Explaining that he had worked with a man called Lucking, Doran talked at length about the years when he served his time in painting and decorating. He told her how he was later given the opportunity to train in the art of signwriting. Producing many high quality signs and wall paintings while in Crewe, he utilised his developing artistic skills where situations allowed. His work at that time was mainly for commercial purposes. Becoming proficient at lettering firms' vans, his signs and motifs could once be admired on numerous sites and vehicles throughout the English town. On the death of his employer, Willie was invited to stay on and continue the reputable business which had been built up. He could have enjoyed a very successful career there as a sign writer. The advantages of living in England were good at that time and there were benefits to be derived by those with talent. He chose instead to follow the prompting of his heart and returned to Ireland in 1962, to live the life of an artist in his home village and to enhance his native surroundings with his acquired expertise.

The conversation had awoken many recollections of the past, including fond memories of the years Willie spent in Crewe, with members of his own family who lived there. He had stayed in digs belonging to relatives of his cousin, Billy Mc Laughlin and later shared the home of his brother Joe. He was reminded also, that another very significant period in his early life was surely those years in Dublin, during the Thirties, because that was the time when he received the greatest influence which had formed him into the artist he had since become.

Through the foresight of Mrs Young, in seeking to advance his education and through the good fortune to have been under the guidance of a painter of the stature of Sarah Purser, Willie knew that he had been given a unique chance in life. He also knew that it was because he had been the recipient of innate and special gifts, that he had been found worthy of such a privilege. He had therefore undertaken to spend the latter years of his lifetime perfecting those skills, in which he had been first trained in his youth and which were always closest to his heart. These were the skills of the landscape painter and they would be placed, first and foremost, at the service of the land in which he was born and which he had always loved passionately.

The young woman was to learn that her neighbour in Culdaff had indeed been associated with a place which would become noted in the history of art, during a time when Irish stained glass was experiencing an important revival. The first few decades of the Twentieth Century told a significant chapter in the story of how Irish stained glass took its place among the best being produced internationally. An Túr Gloine was one of the leading competitors of its day in Dublin, receiving commissions from churches and other important secular buildings, not only in Ireland, but in many other parts of the world. The several diverse artists, who were members of the co-operative, produced during their careers, some of the finest quality stained glass to be found in their own country and beyond, for many centuries.

Coming from a background which had provided little or no facilities for a young man to develop artistic talent, Willie was suddenly catapulted, in 1936, into surroundings where he could learn from and experience at first hand, artists of the highest calibre in their field. His attendance at the College of Art, under instruction by such fine painters and teachers as Keating and Mc Gonigal, laid a strong foundation for him in the training of his own natural ability. Doran's involvement in the studios of An Túr Gloine gave him much insight into the area of stained glass and the high level of skill and endurance which is required to produce work of exception in that medium. He enjoyed the opportunity of meeting and working alongside several gifted artists during the course of only a few years.

An Túr Gloine, in translation, The Tower of Glass, was founded in 1903 and was in the latter years of its existence, with Sarah Purser as director, when Willie went to Dublin. The opening of the studios, brought about through the influence of the great Celtic revivalist, Edward Martyn, had been part of a response to the need to provide good quality church art in Ireland at that time. It naturally also coincided with the introduction of classes in the Metropolitan School of Art to teach the subject. The leading English stained glass artist of the late Nineteenth and early Twentieth centuries, Christopher Whall, was of immense influence to the education of the Irish in this field. It was one of Whall's former students, Alfred Earnest Child, who was invited to the Metropolitan School of Art to introduce there the important discoveries of his prestigious teacher. Alfred E. Child was also appointed as manager of An Túr Gloine and worked in both capacities over the following three decades, personally creating many fine windows for buildings throughout the country and abroad. As a teacher, Child instructed numerous students in the early years of the century. Among those were Beatrice Elvery, later known as Lady Glenavy, Catherine O' Brien, Ethel Rhind and Wilhelmina Geddes, each of whom was invited by Sarah Purser to become a member of the Dublin co-operative. Harry Clarke, the most gifted stained glass artist in Ireland in his day and whose family's studios were the principal competitors of An Túr Gloine, also studied under Child. Clarke's innovative techniques were assimilated by and influenced much of the work of his contemporaries.

Michael Healy was the first artist invited to join An Túr Gloine in 1903. He was in his sixty-third year when Willie Doran met him. His reputation in stained glass had developed steadily by that time. He worked slowly and with meticulous attention to his craft. During the four years that Willie spent in Dublin,

Healy actually produced some of his best work. In 1936, he was completing an impressive Ascension window for Loughrea Cathedral in County Galway, a building which gives testimony to many of the artist's great achievements. By 1937, he had finished working on another, equally distinctive I H S Sacred Heart window. It was one of a series produced by the artists of An Túr Gloine for William Henry Brophy College in Phoenix, Arizona. During the latter years of the Thirties, Healy worked on what was to be his final great window, Last Judgement, again in Loughrea Cathedral. His late work shows a technique which had developed from a masterful ability as a draughtsman to a daring exploitation of colour and composition in glass. Michael Healy died unexpectedly in 1941, while he was still actively involved in pursuing significant projects.

The work of the Dublin artist and his deep spirituality made an enduring impression on the young Doran. To learn from and assist him during the time of his greatest success was indeed an honour. Healy's line drawings and his interest in portraying the lives of the people on the streets of his native Dublin, influenced Willie's habit of observing and recording his own surroundings and the characters who lived there. A lover of sound craftsmanship, Michael Healy was to prove a lasting example to the Donegal man in the meticulous attention he showed to individual details within each composition he produced. Willie practised a similar precise attention to minute detail in all his own endeavours, throughout his life.

As well as experiencing the epitome of Healy's career, Willie was privileged to have been present, in the studios, for the brief membership there of the other artist who was to become a leading exponent of creativity in stained glass, during her lifetime. That was Evie Hone. Already well established as a painter, Evie Hone, together with her friend, the artist Mainie Jellett, had made important advances in the area of abstract composition. She was introduced initially to the craft of stained glass by Wilhelmina Geddes, who was, by the early Thirties, working in London. Evie

Hone was deeply religious and was inspired by early Christian art and Medieval Irish stone carving. This, coupled with an extraordinary use of colour, influenced her to produce a very personal style of work. She became recognised eventually as one of the most original and expressive stained glass artists of the mid-Twentieth Century.

Joining An Túr Gloine in 1933, she remained there until 1944. It was Willie's pleasure to work with her during the central years of her involvement in the Dublin studios, where she carried out several commissions of note. One of these included the large composition, My Four Green Fields, made for the New York World Fair of 1939. It was an exciting time for a young man to be learning from such a distinguished group of people and Doran was even more fortunate that the years he spent there were so significant in the lives of two of its most renowned members.

Evie Hone later moved her practice to a studio at her home in Marlay Grange, Rathfarnham, where she was chosen, from among the top artists of her day, to design and execute the huge east window of Eton College Chapel in England. Depicting The Crucifixion and Last Supper, the commission gained her international recognition. That work took place some time after his stay in Dublin but Willie had taken note of it. He remembered that he had felt a deep sense of pride, on reading about the achievements of a lady who had been so inspirational in his youth and who, in spite of physical difficulties, had become such a creative force in the country.

To be there during this important time had been a rich and diverse experience. To assist with the production of work and to witness the practice of exceptional people at first hand, was a rare opportunity for any developing artist and a lasting example for Willie Doran of the highest levels of achievement that are possible in a field of artistic creation. By 1936, the co-operative had undergone changes in its membership. Most of the original artists had remained there since the early years while others, such as Beatrice Elvery had left in 1912. Wilhelmina Geddes had gone in 1922 and was continuing to achieve success in London. Hubert Mc Goldrick had joined in 1920 and was working there in Willie's time.

Sarah Purser was already fifty-five years old when she had founded the co-operative and was therefore the grand age of eighty-eight when she had extended her generosity to the youth from Culdaff. A successful portrait painter throughout her lifetime, her sitters had included W. B Yeates, Maud Gonne and Douglas Hyde. She was still extremely active, producing many fine works in her latter years with admirable speed and competence. She had organised and held her first one-woman exhibition at the age of seventy-five and did not retire from the running of the studios until 1940, when she was ninety-two. Throughout her long life she was active in Irish cultural affairs. At Mespil House, the mansion where she lived, she held regular discussion gatherings of a wide circle of prominent people, drawn from many walks of life at the time, public, artistic and literary. While he was in Dublin, Willie had visited Mespil on several occasions and even became friendly with some members of the household there. He remembered with fondness walking in the lush gardens of the stately home.

The few years that he spent in An Túr Gloine, although a highly productive era, were also the years which would herald the end of the co-operative. After three successful decades, time and its consequences brought inevitable change. Ethel Rhind retired in 1939. That year also saw the death of the studio's manager, Alfred E. Child. Sarah Purser retired in 1940, after a lifetime devoted to promoting the artistic affairs of the country. Hubert Mc Goldrick and Catherine O'Brien maintained the studios for a few years after Miss Purser's retirement but the final dissolution of the co-operative occurred when Sarah Purser died in 1943. Although Miss O'Brien still produced stained glass there until 1963, the great years of An Túr Gloine were over.

The retirement of his elderly sponsor was preceded by the declaration of the Second World War and the national Emergency. Throughout the country, people were beginning to feel the effect of imposed restrictions. The changed circumstances in the studios meant that there was no longer a job there for Willie and he had to return home. As a result, he could not complete his formal training in the College of Art, which had been on a part-time basis. That was a great regret to him because he knew it could have led, through time, to a recognised qualification. But it was not to be. Years of change were under way and future career prospects would have to be forged now by his own endeavours.

Coming back to Culdaff, he had pursued his interest in landscape and figure study, as well as exploring, in a small way, the area of craft work. There was little or no income to be made from painting in Inishowen then and alternative work had to be acquired again locally. The outbreak of war meant that he would remain at home for a period of eight more years. England was the natural choice for emigration in those days but not many from the area ventured there to seek employment until the war was over. Willie worked for some time with a neighbour, Eddie O' Connor, producing various craft pieces. These they marketed with some success, but his youthful talents would not reach fruition for two more decades, when his adventures in both two and three dimensions would at last receive just acclaim. By 1948, he was ready to leave for England and the security of a trade, in a town where some of his countrymen had already settled and made connections.

The influence of An Túr Gloine left its mark on Willie Doran for many years to come and eventually influenced his decision to return to his native peninsula, after a period of emigration, to pursue a career as a painter. Treasures from the famous studios would also continue to play a part in the religious heritage of Donegal, down through the century and beyond, as a number of fine examples of stained glass had found a place in churches within the county. Some were installed during the early years, while others were produced, by its members, in the decades following the dissolution of the co-operative.

In Inishowen, a small window by Evie Hone, dating from the

late Forties, can be found in St Mura's church in the village of Fahan, along the shores of Lough Swilly. She also created a beautiful circular window for the Catholic church in Ardara, in 1954. Two colourful, opus sectile, war memorial plaques by Catherine O Brien were installed in St Buadan's church in Culdaff village, in 1947. Opus sectile was a type of glass mosaic work which was carried out by some of the artists and featured particularly in depictions of the Stations of the Cross, in churches throughout the country. A window by Alfred E. Child, dating from 1905, can be found in Carndonagh and one by Catherine O Brien, from the 1950s, is to be seen in Buncrana.

Further afield, work by the artists had been selected during the construction of St Eunan's Cathedral in Letterkenny. Michael Healy created the large Drumceat rose window there in 1910, showing an incident from the life of St Columbkille, as well as other windows of saints, including two tiny but excellent ones of St Hugh and St Ann. There are windows there also by A. E. Child, Catherine O'Brien and Beatrice Elvery which were produced in 1911. The ancient Cathedral in Raphoe contains works by Catherine O'Brien and Ethel Rhind, dating from 1906. A small window in it was designed by Sarah Purser herself.

Willie was well aware of the fine legacy which surrounded him. His own parish church, St Mary's, boasted four very good examples of stained glass. They had been installed during the 1930s and were executed by the firm of Earley. Their vibrant colour and graceful composition displays the influence of the high quality work that was being produced in Ireland, during those years. Windows by artists from An Túr Gloine and the studios of Harry Clarke could once be seen on public display in Dublin and in exhibitions in England and America, prior to their installation in buildings abroad, or in other parts of the country. The standard that was being achieved, by the revival in stained glass then, could be experienced widely and greatly influenced the approaches of other craftspeople.

The tall images, in the interior of the chapel at Bocan, never failed to remind Willie of the highly skilled art of which he had been a part. He often reflected on how the creativity which he had witnessed in the stimulating environment of An Túr Gloine, must have had a profound effect on him, as he strove to develop his own talents in later life, without the buoyancy of like-minded people for support. Perhaps it was the dedication of those artists, towards the achievement of superior ideals, that had become his anchor in the often demanding trials of his mature career.

The conversation in the pub had continued until late and Willie Doran had spent a long time sitting at the bar, thinking back over the various topics that had been covered during the course of the evening. Fired strangely by the recollection of his own early experiences, together with some thoughts that he had been having recently, about the growing body of work which had been produced by himself over the past two decades, Willie had suggested to his young friend the possibility of a shared exhibition.

She had recently graduated and there were a few other aspiring painters in the area, whom he was sure would be keen to get together with them, to host a group exhibition. It would be a challenge, but he felt he was, at last, ready to show his work to an interested public, within the local area. They had discussed some possibilities and she seemed enthusiastic. He was becoming quite excited now by the prospect. It would be strange to gather together his own output, to view in its entirety. As nearly all his paintings to date had been on a commissioned basis, Willie had never experienced the luxury of a complete viewing. The young woman would later consider a similarity in his offer to the type of generosity which had once been extended to himself. The Dublin portrait painter had given of the bounty of her resources, to educate a fellow from Inishowen who showed the potential to succeed. Now, the painter of Inishowen was prepared to give of the benefit of his achievements and show his life's work beside the raw efforts of a younger generation. The spirit of co-operative endeavour, she realised, would always be close to his heart.

Willie had left unusually late that night. In fact, he had stayed so long that the pub was empty again by the time he made for home. He had enjoyed their conversation and the awakening of memories, which he recognised had lain hidden, possibly for too long, over the years. The street had been silent as he walked back, quietly relieved that he had not noticed the long hours passing. He felt strangely elated at the prospect of an exhibition. Maybe, he reflected with a hint of nostalgia that Sunday morning, as he washed a few dishes that had been collected from the breakfast table, he was taking a leaf out of the great lady, Sarah Purser's book, when she had held her first solo exhibition in her seventies.

" I might even make it a few years earlier," he smiled gleefully to himself. "Nothing's impossible," Willie thought, as he placed the kettle, filled with fresh water, back onto the range to boil. The kettle spluttered noisily on top of the black, shiny surface. He lifted the grey, aluminium teapot and walked to the back yard, emptying its cold contents into a reserved corner of the grass.

7. School Days
1920s

8. Willie Doran at An Túr Gloine Stained Glass Works,
Dublin 1938
Left to Right: Charles Williams,
Miss Catherine O' Brien, Willie Doran

9. Willie Doran at An Túr Gloine
1938

10. Willie Doran at Mespil House,
home of Sarah Purser 1937

11. With the cook at Mespil House
1937

12. With Charles Williams at the
Stained Glass Works
1937

13. In his workshop in Crewe
1950s

14. Painting a sign in Crewe
1950s

15. Cooper at work c1930s
Pencil

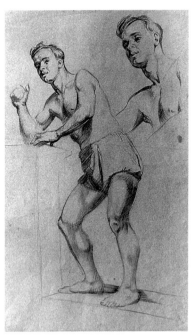

16. Life study, male figure c1930s
Pencil

17. Cobbler at work c1930s
Pencil

18. Portrait of a man smoking a pipe c1930s
Pencil

19. "Why didn't you open the other end ?"
1960s
Pen and Ink

20. "Got yer this time, Mr flipping Picasso !"
1950s
Pen and Ink

CHAPTER FOUR
A Talent for Caricature

The clock ticked quietly as the day hurried by. It was nearly twelve and people were eventually up and about. Willie had gone down the street to buy a newspaper in one of the shops, which was busy now with customers on their way home from the second Mass. Glancing at the time showing on the small, round face above the mantle piece, he settled down to read.

There was a football match that afternoon, in a field close by, which served as the local pitch. He would sit for a while, he thought, before making the dinner. Not being particularly hungry at that moment, his meal could wait until later. Some bacon and cabbage would be quickly fried and eaten before leaving the house. Bacon and cabbage was always tasty with a few potatoes and Willie enjoyed a fry. Maybe he would have time later for a quick cycle to the shore, if the weather stayed fine. It had been fairly mild so far this year, but December was a cold month and the darkening sky was showing some unmistakable signs of rain.

Leafing through the newspaper, he caught sight of a political cartoon. Poking fun at a situation, which happened to be in the news that weekend, a cartoonist had brought a wry message to bear about the topical event. Smiling to himself, Willie noted the exaggerated features and clever effects that had been achieved in the tiny drawing, with a minimum use of black ink. A lively play on words, summing up the incident in a concise but appropriate caption, completed the clever statement. Doran loved the visual wit of the cartoonist. In addition to his capability in painting, he was blessed with a real gift for that art form himself. While living in England in the 1950s, he had worked hard at developing his ability in the area of caricature. It was a type of work he enjoyed immensely and having a natural facility, his talent was put to use regularly for his own amusement. Many drawings were produced during spare hours there and submitted for publication to local newspapers. He achieved a respectable level of success in this highly competitive field, but it was an aspect of the artist's work which was, above all, produced for his own personal pleasure and enjoyment.

Combining excellent draughtsmanship with a finely honed sense of humour, Willie Doran's early cartoons display a keen observation of urban life. He drew bus queues full of city types, dazed boxers in a ring and a large, fierce butcher in a striped apron, wielding a cleaver as he chases a young street urchin who has scribbled crude pictures of the angry man on the heavy wooden door of his shop. A thin faced lodger was created, seated at the breakfast table and discovering to his horror a live chicken in an innocent looking boiled egg! Figures and incidents were inspired by the experiences he encountered while working in England and were then heavily embroidered with his natural sense of humour and a quick ability with words. While absorbing the life of his surroundings in Crewe, he also delved into a bank of memories, that were stored in his mind, of familiar faces from home. He produced numerous pen and ink cartoons when in England and continued to work, for a time, in the medium after he returned to Culdaff.

An exaggerated nose and elongated neck, a gaping mouth or flyaway tufts of hair on a balding scalp; a boy's skinny legs appearing out of a pair of huge shorts, all expertly drawn, became increasingly recognisable as his personal trademarks. Including many facets of the human condition that had been observed during his boyhood, Willie cleverly adapted and combined innumerable variations within characters, in pursuit of the ultimate comic statement. Political satire, as well as scenes from everyday life was portrayed at that time, his enthusiastic attitude to politics being successfully depicted and always very aptly captioned.

There was another memorable type of pen and watercolour study produced during those years. On a few occasions, he portrayed a number of delightful and funny scenes, in which actual people from his home village were shown. These intimate works were painted, not for publication, but as personalised Christmas cards which were sent home to friends while he was abroad. Neighbours and recognisable personalities featured in the paintings which, although created from a distance, showed accurate attention to minute details that had been fondly remembered from daily life in Inishowen. The Christmas cards were dispatched, over a few years, to some of his friends, two of whom were Neal Lynch and his brother Patrick, known locally as Fredrick. The imagined frolics of village inhabitants brought many hours of laughter and enjoyment to all back at home in Donegal. Humorously and very cleverly composing hilarious scenes of Christmas revelry, enacted by the local community in caricature, Culdaff was brought to life for himself as he sat in Crewe, lovingly drawing and painting the inspired works.

Willie often longed, during those years, to be reunited with his old friends and looked forward to the day when he would sit at home and observe his neighbours, once again, in their native environment. On his return in 1962, he continued to draw the people of the village. More often then however, he sketched privately, noting passers by on the road with a quick stroke of his pen. Less cartoons were produced over the years as other activities began to take up more of his time. Commissions for paintings and a consistent demand for his decorating skills had ensured a busy schedule during the past two decades.

There was one type of interior decorating work, in which he became involved, where Doran was able to make use of his figurative skills to great advantage. This was in the field of mural painting. He was requested, by a number of people in the local business community, to carry out a range of murals on the interior walls of public premises around Inishowen. Brendan Faulkner, an enterprising businessman from Culdaff, was the first to avail of Willie's expertise in this area, when he opened a small dance hall locally. In response, some fine work was carried out on alcoves within the hall, when it originally came into use. An interesting environment was created for the interior, where painted stone borders framed a series of imaginary windows displaying colourful landscape views.

One of the murals there featured a painting of a bog land scene. It showed a boy bringing home a donkey, laden with turf, along a rough mountain road. An unusually high horizon, against which to show the figures was chosen, capturing the dramatic and bleak effect of a wet, bog road, lit by the gentle light of a rainy evening in Donegal. The scene was somewhat reminiscent of work by Sean Keating. Keating's paintings of the people who lived on the Aran Islands during the early years of the century, display a sincere empathy with his subjects and the difficulty of their lives on the inhospitable, western seaboard. The experience of working on a similar type of subject, at that time, gave Willie the chance to explore an image, typical of many which he had witnessed in his own surroundings, as a boy in north Donegal. He composed the familiar event with an instinctive feeling for the hard toil of the subjects portrayed. It was the only figurative subject, among the other landscape scenes provided for the little hall, but it was a particularly successful endeavour with which both artist and patron had been justly pleased.

Brendan Faulkner opened a larger ballroom called 'The Culdaff Arms', some years later. It became noted as one of the top dance venues in Inishowen, during the final years of the 1960s and the early 1970s. Once again he engaged the local artist to decorate. This time the more economic style of his cartoon work was chosen to create lively, monochromatic paintings of various recreational items around the walls of the building. The adapted style befitted the modern function of the new ballroom, where the emphasis had, by then, shifted to the use of strong lighting to create colour and decoration on a darkened dance floor. The walls needed to be left light and airy, but lively enough to inspire a feeling of fun. Champagne glasses, sparkling bottles and a variety of dancing forms were painted, creating fitting images for a background to musical entertainment, within a tall, spacious interior. This minimal approach was much enjoyed by the young patrons who frequented the lively centre.

Adapting easily to the demands of each interior he was asked to decorate, Willie was always open to new situations, accepting readily the challenges of every individual's requirements. He created numerous murals for Mc Grory's Hotel in Culdaff over the years, most of which were inspired by landscape rather than figurative themes. He also produced an excellent, large, wall painting for Malin Hotel, depicting the spectacular local landscape of Trawbreaga Bay, stretching out before the encircling hills of Inishowen and the familiarity of a small, thatched cottage nestling by the water's edge. Farming activity, that was typical of the area at that time, included a man following a plough drawn by two sturdy horses and a rooster chasing a hen through the field. The scene was set under a rosy sky, against which a flock of birds flew in formation to some exotic destination. Willie was at his most relaxed when painting landscape but he readily accepted difficult and sometimes unusual commissions with a spirit of optimistic endeavour. The enjoyment he found in including humorous characters in a scene, allowed him an occasional adventure.

One remarkable piece of mural work, where he was able to give free reign to his skills in comic figure composition, was carried out in the old coach house of Redcastle Hotel. The building is set on an estate beside the shores of Lough Foyle. A history of the estate includes many stories of incidents where horses and coaches have had a prominent role. When asking for a mural to be created, high up near the ceiling of the coach house, which was being converted into a night club, the management decided that an appropriate theme should reflect something of the historic background of the building, while addressing its contemporary function as a leisure facility. Doran obliged by creating a unique centrepiece comprising two scenes, which successfully combined the building's history with an element of comedy. Using his expertise in drawing, an eye catching drama was composed.

On one side an overloaded coach was shown, pulled wearily by struggling horses, with a little driver perched aloft on his rickety seat. The coach appeared to be heading dangerously towards a stream but the passengers seemed oblivious to the precarious situation. The other side showed the scene after an inevitable disaster had occurred. The horses had stumbled, the driver had been flung over them and the coach had collapsed, leaving a trail of chaos behind. All was mayhem, a cartoonist's paradise! He had worked long at that piece and thoroughly enjoyed the challenge of such a large and complicated commission. Young people, who danced weekly in the venue, would admire, for years, the skill of an artist who had created such a fine storyboard above their heads. It never failed to provide amusement for all who looked up during a quiet moment on a Saturday night out.

The Inishowen painter had always taken great delight in introducing elements of humanity into his landscape or feature work, when an opportunity arose. Brian Bonner, the respected historian and scholar from Culdaff, had, the previous year, commissioned an oil painting of two, locally sited, early Christian crosses at Carrowmore. The ancient crosses are in separate fields with a narrow road running between them. They were once part of the monastery of Both Chonais, forming just two of the many structures to be found within the Sixth century enclosure.

Willie had cycled the few miles one day to Carrowmore, to make some studies in watercolour as a preparation for his painting. He always prepared carefully for each commission and cycled to all nearby locations, so that he could adequately study the elements of his compositions in their outdoor setting. Noting the grey forms and roughening textures of the crosses, in part still displaying traces of ancient carving, he had felt a lovely sense of peace in the area. Somehow, sitting alone, at work in the field there, austere in its silence that day, he became aware of experiencing a hub of activity from the past.

Once a vital part of the spiritual life of the peninsula, the monastery's history had become condensed now into a small fragment of what remained of its original enclosure, two silent crosses standing separately in two lonely fields. In his mind's eye, he visualised the scene which must have been witnessed there centuries before, when monks were going about their work and prayer. There would have been walls, he thought and a church must have stood somewhere within the area where he was now sitting. There may have been buildings like a scriptorium, where passages from the Gospels would have been faithfully recorded and decorated. Little beehive huts must have been dotted around the enclosure, where the monks could sleep and pray. Willie had been requested by the historian, not to show the crosses in their present isolation, but to place them within an imaginary setting which would contain features of their original location and purpose. As he sat there that afternoon, a composition became clear to him.

When completed, the large painting consisted, not only of the two crosses in the foreground, but it also showed three tiny beehive huts behind. Coming through the rocks and grass beyond, was a procession of five brown-habited monks, making their way to rest or for prayer. Set into either side, at the base, were further panels depicting two local figures, Comghall and Maol Iosa. The use of an inset was a technique which Willie adapted easily from his experience of working in stained glass composition. There, small panels are often inserted into a larger picture to enhance the telling of an elaborate story, within the confines of a single window. Writing their names and that of the monastery 'Both Chonais' in a neat Irish script, a device also used earlier in the century, by stained glass artists, he gave title to a famous place.

The painting was very much appreciated by Brian Bonner when it was presented to him. The artist's ingenuity had provided a unique visual insight into a local place of great historic importance. This was of special interest to a scholar who had written many fine books about his native peninsula and the rich cultural and religious heritage that it possessed.

Many of the commissions, undertaken by Willie Doran, reflected the frequent requests he had received to portray both people and places of significance. Over the years, he had been asked to record, pictorially, a number of buildings that were dear to families for one reason or another. Sometimes it was an ancient homestead which had fallen into ruin, or had been so renovated that much of the original character had been lost. At other times, he would be asked to paint a farm house that had once been the home of someone now living abroad. He ingeniously recreated the character of many traditional homesteads and even some larger houses and estates, often bringing them to life by the inclusion of a familiar human or animal presence. There were numerous examples of commissions, around Inishowen and in other parts of the country, where Willie had reproduced, very successfully, a vivid reminder of the original appearance of a long remembered home.

One interesting project, which he had undertaken recently, was a painting of the early thatched building, which once housed the pub owned by Simpsons of Carndonagh. Their new premises had been renovated considerably over the years and would probably continue to change greatly in the future. The Simpson family wanted a record of where it all began and Willie was requested to provide the image. He produced a lasting portrait for the owners, which they proudly displayed in their newly refurbished bar, perfectly reflecting the character of the old dwelling which had been in existence at the outset of their business. Encapsulating an interesting piece of local history, it would continue to remind patrons of the vast changes which had taken place in the development of Inishowen pubs, over the years.

Sometimes the Culdaff artist was given photographs, many of inferior quality, from which to produce a portrait of a person. Subjects were often people from an earlier generation who had died. Occasionally he had to work from a faded, brown stained image which may have been the only remaining record of a relative, dating back to an age when photography was in its infancy. Almost miraculously, in every case, he would construct a striking likeness from even the poorest of prints, bringing a welcome and lasting remembrance to the family of a person who had gone.

The portrait was always a challenge. Willie enjoyed sitting at home, on a winter evening, drawing his own likeness as it stared back at him from a mirror on the kitchen table. Having studied his face on numerous occasions, many pages in sketchbooks showed a changing countenance, reflected in the same mirror, as the years progressed. Using himself as the subject, a range of approaches to drawing and painting the portrait were continually explored and then employed confidently in his larger studies and oil paintings of other people.

Recently, from memory, he had sketched his mother. Remembering her sitting in the kitchen, playing the melodeon, he had made a pen drawing of her in a note book. Willie searched for a moment among a few papers that were neatly stacked on a shelf in the cupboard close by. Finding the little sketch pad, he flicked the pages slowly, till he reached the one where her image had been drawn. The fondly constructed figure of his mother, with a melodeon on her knee, reminded him suddenly of the other members of the Mc Laughlin family, to whom she had belonged and who had lived near him in Culdaff, throughout the preceding decade. They were all dead now but over the years, since he came home, they had been a strong and abiding presence in his life.

The Mc Laughlins had a great tradition in cycling. No wonder he was so fond of the bike himself, Willie often thought. His uncles, Jim and Eddie, had won competitions throughout the country and their brother, Barney, had also cycled competitively in America. He remembered drawing a portrait of his uncle, Jim Mc Laughlin. A tall, straight figure of a man, Jim fixed bicycles for years, in the top storey of a building which stood at the bottom of the village green. The building was called the Loan Fund, as it had once been a place in which money was loaned to the people of the area. Although its function had changed over the years, the long, tall building had still not lost its original title among the older inhabitants. Willie had often watched Jim coming up the street, managing two bicycles at one time, as he brought a spare one back to the workshop beside the house where the family lived. The house was some way up the Moville Road, on the outskirts of the village. Jim would cycle on one bicycle while guiding the other with his free hand. This feat, which often mesmerised the local children, was not a difficult task for a man who had raced bicycles in his youth. It was the youthful Jim Mc Laughlin whom Willie had sketched in pencil, by his bike, dressed in cycling gear and caught during a proud moment. Sarah, his aunt, had cherished the drawing, proud of her brother's achievements, for which the house held many trophies, but also proud of the young son of her sister, Cassie, who was able to portray the champion in such a fine manner.

The four Mc Laughlins who had remained unmarried, lived at the edge of the village throughout their last years, two brothers and two sisters, sharing a home until they died. Eddie was a lively man up to the age of eighty, when he could cycle and walk as well as any young fellow in the district. He was also skilled in drawing. Fannie was the post-woman for years around Culdaff. His father's brother, Christy Doran, was a post-man. They travelled miles every day, on foot or by bicycle, delivering letters. Sarah looked after the house and was a friendly sort. She was artistic in her own way also and had great time for children.

Willie left the small book down, emotion welling even yet inside him when he thought of his own people. His father had been in the Merchant Navy when they were young and was away at sea for much of their childhood. As the eldest, he had been very close to his mother and remembered the wrench it was for both of them when he had to bid her leave to go to Dublin. It was important that people should be remembered, he thought and Willie hoped that he had been the bearer of joy to some families over the years, through the respectable number of portraits he had painted.

21. Memory sketch of Kathleen Doran playing the melodeon
1979
Pen and Ink

22. Madaleine knitting
1978
Pencil

Two memorable images stood out in his mind. They were among his most successful portraits, in his opinion, although each was significant in its own right. One was a portrayal of the late Mrs Edward Henry O' Doherty, a well-respected music teacher from Derry. The distinguished lady was the mother of Mrs Josephine Devlin, wife of Doctor Joe Devlin, who lived and practised in Derry. The Devlins spent their summer holidays in Culdaff and when they arrived, they became Willie's neighbours. Theirs was a large family and they stayed in one of the tall, semi-detached houses to the left of his home. The house became full of activity during July and August. On request from the family, Willie had painted a small but exquisite portrait of Mrs Rose O' Doherty, in which he had captured a great sense of the warmth and vitality of his subject. This was achieved particularly through the fine treatment of her eyes, which glowed with life and a soft expression of enduring humanity. It was a fitting tribute to a lady, who had been instrumental in promoting the love of music in so many people, down through the years.

The other portrait was one which had made a profound impact on himself. It had been produced only recently and was a study of the saintly Padre Pio. Commissioned from a local patron, he had undertaken the painting in his usual way, working from a popular photograph of the famous priest. It was still in his house, awaiting collection. Willie had encountered an experience while carrying out that portrait, the memory of which made him feel rather strange. He received a distinct feeling, while working on the painting, that nothing could possibly go wrong with its execution. The brush in his hand, he recalled, had seemed to move as if guided by a kind of heavenly force. It was a unique experience and not one which was likely to be repeated. Willie had never been given to fanciful notions but he could not deny what had happened. He was aware that the priest from San Giovanni was reputed for many unusual occurrences, during his life and since his death and this had been a gratifying reward for a painter whose art was always at the service of his faith. On showing the finished work to a friend, Willie had acknowledged, privately, the unusual happening. He had confided then also that the portrait of Padre Pio was the best that he had produced during his entire career.

Doran's output in portraiture extended beyond the bounds of easel painting. A recent commission had been carried out for the parish of Culdaff the previous September. It was the creation of a banner for the visit of Pope John Paul 11 to Ireland. The banner was brought to Galway by the young people of the parish, during the visit of the Pope there. In this work, past and present were again successfully combined. An ancient Mass rock was shown. Before it a priest, from the days of the Penal Laws in Ireland, celebrated Mass. The image was borrowed from a similar subject which he had explored in his youth, but this time the historic backdrop was set beside a lively portrait of the newly elected Pope. Contrasting the hidden celebrations of the faith of past generations, with the freedom in which the present Holy Father could be welcomed into the country, a powerful composition had been created. Small panels, showing historic Christian and pre-Christian sites from around the parish, were also included. It was an impressive piece, depicting the enduring faith of an area which is steeped in a tradition of both ancient mystery and Christian worship. Many people admired his work in Galway. The banner was displayed in the local church for some time afterwards and parishioners, who had not been involved in the visit, could see at first hand, an example of the skill and vision of the accomplished artist who lived so quietly in their midst.

Willie eventually turned his attention back to the open page of the Sunday newspaper. It had been left idle on his knee, while his mind wandered back, again and again, through a plethora of memories that had been aroused by glancing at the small cartoon. He lifted his glasses from the table where they had been laid earlier, as he continued to recall people and places which had featured prominently in his life. It was a good life, he thought. Willie loved the little village of Culdaff with its proximity to the sea and the gently rising hills that surrounded it. He had spoken, on rare occasions, of the great fondness he had for his native environment, admitting that it pained him severely to see even a single tree in any way damaged or destroyed. He had often reminded himself, as the years went by in England, that every day spent away from Ireland was for him, as an artist, an important day missed. Notwithstanding the valuable training and experience received while in Crewe, his heart was always in Inishowen and he knew that the decision to return home when he did had been the right one.

He had certainly wasted no time since coming back. By now a substantial output of work had been produced, which he genuinely felt would be interesting to acknowledge in retrospect. His mind turned to thoughts of a forthcoming exhibition. It was an exciting prospect, he had to admit and he had many ideas in his head for the suggestion which had been mooted to his young neighbour the other night. If he could harness the enthusiasm of the up and coming generation, they could, together, create a very successful venture, he felt sure. However, being modest and unobtrusive by nature, the older man knew that he would never impose his ideas on anyone and decided to wait and see what further discussions brought forth.

Putting his glasses back on, Willie rose from the seat and walked out to the door. He stood there for a while, taking in the cool, December air. The sky had become very cloudy in the past hour and he wondered if it would stay dry for the match. Standing, with one arm leaning on the door post, as was his habit, he spotted the young woman going down the street.

"This would be a good time to show her the painting," he thought. "I'll give her a shout."

She was taking her niece to the shop and they seemed preoccupied, as she tried vainly to keep the child at her side from running out onto the road. Seeing Willie at the door, she stopped for a few minutes to talk, by the side of the green. The conversation was brief that morning, as her eyes flicked constantly to the welfare of her charge. Eventually, the child was becoming increasingly restless and she made to leave. Taking his chance, Willie asked if she would like to come in and see a picture he had just finished. She hesitated. The toddler was urging her to move and she excused herself politely from his invitation, promising to return sometime later, when she could view the work in peace. Willie Doran's house was no place for a two year old, she had decided, as she said goodbye and walked on down the street, reminding herself to call back in the evening.

Though disappointed, he smiled and accepted the apology. After a while longer at the door, he went inside. It would have been good to show the painting that morning, he thought sadly. He had been so pleased with it earlier and he wanted to share his reaction with someone whom he knew would also be affected by the fine outcome that had been achieved. Would she return that afternoon, he wondered. If she did not call down early, there would be the match to attend and by the time that was over, the street would be in darkness. Pictures always looked better in the morning, he thought. It would have been good to show this one in the daylight.

Willie felt a slight sense of loneliness as he looked around the empty house. To cheer himself up, he began to think about members of his family and the friends who came to visit in the summer. His sister, Veronica, returned home every year with her children. Her daughter, Madaleine, had been coming for holidays since her childhood. He enjoyed great times with them all and he knew that they were also fond of him. Madaleine had photographed him once, at the back door, as he threw scraps of bread onto the tin roof of the shed outside for birds. He had drawn her too, sitting quietly knitting, by the window in his kitchen, the previous year. The warm presence of Veronica's family would fill the house from the moment they arrived. It was good to be together for the holidays. He smiled as he longed for their lively humour that morning.

He thought of Teddy, his nephew, and the enjoyment they both shared for the game of football. Willie's brother Joe and his wife

Susan came into his mind. He had stayed in their home in England many years before. Recently, he had returned to Crewe for the wedding of one of the family. It was great to be reunited, even for a short time, but he only went back to England now to visit. His family had made their homes there and would not be likely to return. Willie knew, in his heart, that his home could only ever be here in Donegal and he thanked God for the kind neighbours and friends who made living alone a little easier.

He had formed a number of good friendships over the years. Cartha Byrne was a regular visitor to his house and was one of the few people in whom he confided his deeper thoughts. Many hours of fine conversation were spent by them in the small kitchen and they discussed a range of subjects with a shared enthusiasm. A friend of the Byrnes for most of his lifetime, having worked with both Tom and Paddy in England, Willie maintained a great loyalty to the Malin family.

Sean and Teresa Farren were two people with whom he had also enjoyed many years of friendship. Sean was from Faherna, a little way beyond Culdaff and his wife was a gentle woman from County Clare. He had become friendly with them while they were working in England and they always renewed their acquaintances when the couple returned on holiday, during the summer months. Sitting down for a moment, Willie chuckled to himself, as he began to recall some of the good times they had spent together over the years. Sean and he had travelled to England on the boat, on several occasions and they shared countless memories of their experiences, good and bad, on the far side of the Irish Sea. Everything came to life when friends arrived, he thought, glancing out the window as a pair of children ran gleefully down the brae, shouting and laughing together, without a care in the world.

Willie always took his holidays to coincide with those of the Farrens. The busy artist allowed himself, once a year, the luxury of an idle fortnight. A jar of coffee was procured, especially for his two guests from England, knowing that they preferred coffee to his usual pot of tea. After an enjoyable night out in one of the local pubs, all three would retire to Dorans' where they would be treated to some of his own homemade, treacle bread. Much time was spent during those nights, talking and joking, often well into the small hours of the morning. Both Sean and Willie possessed the same hearty sense of humour, with which they could keep each other in fits of laughter, for hours on end.

He enjoyed many motor outings when his friends were at home. It was a chance to partake of the luxury of being driven by car and the Farrens always ensured that a few excursions would take place over the fortnight. One time a slight accident was narrowly averted, involving a local character on a bike. True to form, Willie seized on the memory of the incident and produced, months later, a humorous and much exaggerated illustration of the scene. Showing an imaginative depiction of themselves in a car, with the figure of the other fellow and his bike flying up into the air, he captured forever a moment of mirth, which could be enjoyed by many, long after the incident had been forgotten.

Time always passed quickly with fine entertainment and the good company of family and friends, he thought, as he allowed his gaze to dwell briefly on the bare winter trees outside his window and the empty road, bereft again of its laughing children. Looking forward to the summer when the fun could begin once more, he decided he'd better start making the dinner.

"Hunger's a great reminder of the present day," Willie conceded, making his way out into the scullery to prepare something to eat.

Colour Plates

1. Mass Rock in the Penal Days 1940s
Oil 30 x 40 cm

2. Catching sand eels at the Mouth of the River c1940
Watercolour 35 x 44 cm

3. Charlie (Cathal) McLaughlin's Cottage at Trawbreaga Bay 1967
Oil 32 x 46 cm

4. Dunmore Head, Culdaff Bay 1967
Oil 32 x 46 cm

5. Bunagee Pier, Culdaff Bay 1968
Oil   60 x 122 cm

6. Malin Village 1963
Oil   31 x 46.5cm

7. Charlie (Cathal) McLaughlin's Cottage, evening sky 1965
Oil 46 x 74cm

8. Charlie (Cathal) McLaughlin's farm and cottage, Trawbreaga Bay c1965
Oil   122 x 294 cm

9. Mrs Rose O'Doherty *(Edward Henry)*, Derry c1970
Oil   46 x 20 cm
Posthumous Portrait

10. Culdaff Bay 1971
Emulsion 119 x 125 cm
Wall Panel in McGrory's Hotel, Culdaff

11. Mountain Stream 1970
Emulsion
Stage Panel for Mc Grory's Hotel, Culdaff

12. A Lakeside Cottage 1970
Emulsion
Stage Panel for Mc Grory's Hotel, Culdaff

13. A Donegal Homestead 1974
Turf carving Acrylic finish

14. An Irish Clachan 1963
Turf carving Watercolour finish

15. Culdaff Village in the Sixties 1973
Oil 61 x 87 cm
Sergeant Mc Donagh and Tommy Wilkie are walking up the street.
Lynch's bread-van is parked outside Brodbins' shop.

16. Chapel at Lagg c1975
Oil 36 x 45 cm

17. Simpsons' Bar, Tul na Rí, Carndonagh 1976
Oil   69 x 91 cm

18. McColgans' Farmhouse (Early Twentieth Century) Corvish, Carndonagh 1975
Oil   67 x 111 cm
Left to Right - Mr McColgan, Isabella McColgan, Michael McColgan

19. Bunagee, Culdaff Bay 1977
Oil   40 x 50 cm

20. The Five Fingers Strand 1977
Oil   50 x 76 cm

21. Both Chonais 450-1350 1978
Oil 87 x 107 cm
Insets : Maol Iosa and Comhgall

22. Cross at Carrowmore 1978
Watercolour 26 x 30 cm

23. Cross and carved stone at Carrowmore 1978
Watercolour 29 x 41 cm

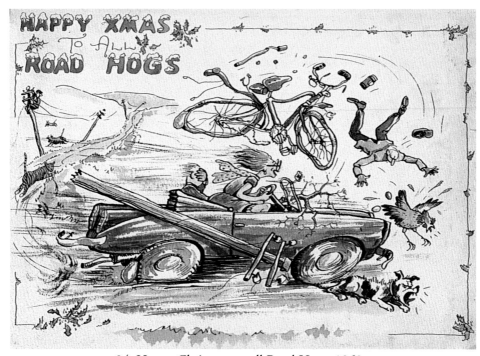

24. Happy Christmas to all Road Hogs 1960s
Watercolour, Pen and Ink   19 x 27 cm

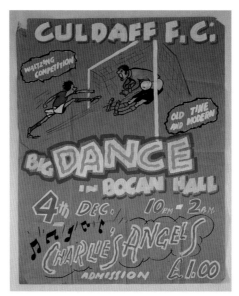

25. Poster for Culdaff Football Club 1970s
Acrylic   72 x 59 cm

26. Tom Grace in Landsdowne Road 1979
Oil   61 x 50 cm
Ireland vs England 1973
Tom Grace capped 25 times for Ireland,
8 as captain of the Irish rugby team (1970 - 78)

27. The Pump, Culdaff Village Green 1979
Watercolour 12 x 17 cm
Dated 13th June 1979
Brodbins' Shop, closed, in the background.

28. Redford Shore 1979
Watercolour 40 x 51 cm
Dated 10th Sept. 1979

29. The Pier, Malin Head 1979
Oil   43 x 61 cm
Willie Doran's last painting - unsigned

30. Evening, Lagg Road 1978
Oil   38 x 43 cm

31. Padre Pio 1979
Oil   61 x 46 cm

23. An Irish Homestead
1950s
Pencil

24. A Donegal Homestead
1960s
Turf carving - Watercolour finish

CHAPTER FIVE
Houses From Turf

Always keen on diversity, Doran's achievements were not confined to the two-dimensional. On a chair inside the kitchen door, partially completed, sat three of his 'wee houses'. This was the name by which the artist jokingly referred to small sculptures of Irish cottages which he carved from turf. Willie had first been attracted to this type of work when he was in Dublin. Having seen some turf carving displayed there, he had decided to experiment with the medium himself. His earliest attempts, begun after he came home in 1940, were brought to a chemist in Derry to sell. They were received with interest in the city then and were also sold, occasionally, in one of the shops in Culdaff.

In addition to developing his career as a painter, he had continued, since 1962, to explore and refine his carving and modelling techniques and had perfected the ability to produce an exact replica of a traditional Irish farmhouse. A journalist once, on hearing about the unique sculptures, wrote an article about this work. During the interview, Willie was asked if he would ever be tempted, by their success, to consider mass production. Adamant that his enjoyment was derived from working on each piece individually, he had insisted then and continued to maintain the belief, that he preferred variety in his work to mass production and enjoyed selling the models, personally, to the occasional tourist who happened to drop in. There was a growing demand from local people also for them because they made an ideal gift for relatives or friends living abroad. As a result, the 'wee houses' could be found in many countries all over the world.

Their official title was *A Donegal Homestead* and they contained, on a miniature scale, all that was to be found in a typical smallholding in rural Donegal. Each one was original in concept, although a similar format was employed to embrace, characteristically, the general feeling of a traditional farmhouse and its surroundings. A single, long sod formed the base of the piece. At times it was necessary to splice two shorter sods and join them together with strong glue. He had access to a good source of black turf from a local bog. These, with some treatment, proved to be ideal for the job. An adequate supply was left in the shed outside to dry. From time to time, he would take the best of them into the back room, off the kitchen, so that they could air out even further. Well shaped sods were then selected in rotation when required.

Willie used a shoemaker's knife to carve the initial shape. At that stage it was often necessary to carry out some repair work, as there would naturally be many imperfections in the fabric of the raw material. Filling and making smooth the surfaces of the structure, he would proceed by using a variety of modelling techniques. The final and most important stage was the painting of the piece and the addition of some minute, expertly constructed farm implements and other features, to enhance the authenticity of the scene.

The complete unit, when finished, comprised a cottage and outbuildings, with a little bit of garden to the side and a front street. The street is the name commonly used in Donegal to denote the area just outside the door of a farmhouse. The first Homesteads produced were plain, long buildings, with the addition of a byre or some outhouses. The few windows incorporated were tiny and the thatch heavy. Their appearance reflected an older style of dwelling, typical of those to be found in the county during the 1940s, when the idea was first conceived. Willie had continued to create that type of cottage until the late Sixties, when he began to change them slightly, in pursuit of nuances in form and decoration. For some years, using a short, broad shaped sod as a base, he had explored the possibility of creating smaller cottages with a more substantial surround. These proved quite popular for a time, but he returned to his original longer forms eventually, finding that it gave him more scope to be creative, with the various individual details that he greatly enjoyed portraying, within the immediate vicinity of the farmyard.

Noticing some novel features, which had been occurring lately in the modernisation of the old dwellings, he had started to introduce new characteristics into his models during the past few years. This included a variety of slated extensions, which were becoming popular in the old buildings, as they made their uneasy progress into the second half of the Twentieth Century. He enjoyed giving his cottages a contemporary feeling and his eye for all sorts of interesting detail, observed on his travels around Inishowen, kept him up to date with a ready supply of inspiration. Recent sculptures were becoming, therefore, a reflection of the modernised, rather than original, thatched cottage.

The colour of his houses had also undergone some differences throughout their development. That had come about for a reason. The change, in the final appearance of later models, had happened as a response to solving the problem of a good finish, which was achieved using acrylic paints. Acrylics were a waterproof alternative to the earlier ones, which had been painted with watercolours. The use of that medium had enhanced the natural look of the pieces but they had presented some difficulty in their care, especially when displayed in dusty conditions. Acrylics gave a slightly brighter finish than the soft hues of watercolour, but were much more easily maintained and permanent. Later cottages, although slightly stronger in colour, retained their subtlety of hue through Willie's well practised mixing techniques.

However they had changed over the years, the Donegal Homesteads were always a delight to behold. There was the familiar thatched roof, sometimes old and worn in appearance and sometimes fresh looking and new. Criss-crossed ropes were finely modelled, slightly raised out from the surface and neatly attached to small, dark hooks, which sat in relief on the gable ends. The heavy, full thatch of the early days had become shorter and smarter. When he introduced a slated roof, it was complete with spout and drainpipe, which emptied into a miniature water barrel at the front of the house. A worn, corrugated iron roof covered the byre. Rusting pink and faded blue shades created a convincing appearance of the effects of weathering, seen on corrugated iron which is under constant punishment from harsh Irish skies. Black paint suggested tar protection on the tops of outhouses.

Tiny, well-formed turf stacks were carved out of the raw turf and left untreated. In the end, this unforgettable feature of any Irish homestead, would be the only recognisable portion of the original material, as everything else became so well finished, it would be difficult to imagine the humble source from which it had been derived. A couple of hay stacks were usually included at the side of the buildings, nestling under the shelter of a low, stone wall. Natural rocks and hillocks of grass were carved, suggesting how the old homes had been built, frequently, in difficult and inhospitable soil, the already existing outcrops becoming a typical feature of their surrounds later. Soft pink and grey colours of stone and rock were contrasted against bright, intermittent flashes of mossy green, to achieve the effect of rugged, natural growth around the house.

Giving attention to exact detail in colour and shape, donkey carts, churns, sticks and hoes were constructed separately from pieces of soft wood. Painted in rich, dark browns, they were neatly attached to the larger area, giving a pleasing touch of activity along the front of the house. Walls were coloured white, suggesting the glow of new whitewash on a summer's day. Borders around windows, sills and the top of a small, protruding porch, sheltering the front door, contrasted sharply in deep red. The sizes and shapes of windows were varied. Newly renovated parts of a house displayed a slightly more modern style than an older section. With minute attention, individual panes of glass were painted with a fine, pointed brush. Up to twelve tiny panes might be drawn onto an area which measured no more than a child's thumbnail in diameter. Doran's skill in working in miniature and the accuracy of his detail added to the quality of his craft work.

Chimney tops showed the effect of smoke soiling. Brown stains trailed partly down gable walls, as obviously as can be seen on a real cottage, where the only source of heat is a constantly burning turf fire. Willie's faithfulness, in the portrayal of a subject which he knew intimately, meant that the models always retained their freshness. Because he took such delight in updating his creations, they never degenerated into a careless or predictable outcome, as can happen easily, when a vast number have been produced over a period of more than twenty years.

Final details were added to suggest a feeling of real life along the farmyard. Plump hens were modelled, poking busily as if for food in the gravel street, which was strewn with a thin layer of sand. With their heads pointing judiciously towards the ground and tail feathers sticking boldly up in the air, the little forms gave the effect of a real brood, scurrying to catch a few grains of corn that would be thrown from a farmhouse door. A splash of red highlighted the combs on their heads as they scattered in different directions. Sometimes a duck pond was carved into the scene, a layer of clear varnish creating a luminous effect. Two or three ducks swam on the calm, shiny surface.

Grasses, collected along the shore road, were dried and stored carefully in large matchboxes. These were used as flowering plants at the front wall of the cottage. With the application of some whitening and paint, they gave a striking impression of wild rose bushes growing there. A hollowed out space behind a brightly coloured half door, hinted at a human presence, about to appear from the darkness of the interior. Byre doors, in fading shades of weathered wood, were left partly open, suggesting a daytime working pattern and animals gone to the fields. A stable was added to denote the specialised requirements of stock. Bits of real hay lay on the floor inside a shed with sloping roof, which completed a range of outhouses.

It was a mark of Willie's inventiveness and skill, that he had reached such a level of achievement in the models. It was also because of his fine painting ability and attention to detail, that the little houses had become such accomplished works of craftsmanship in their own right. He often used to think, as he threw a bit of turf onto the fire, how versatile such a humble material could be. They give us heat. They enable us to cook food. In days gone by, they were even used in the construction of the walls and roofs of some of our homes. Now he had discovered, much to his delight and pleasure over the years, that with a degree of skill and imagination, turf could be used for the making of works of art. It was strange and quite humorous, he often mused, how something as unassuming as a sod of turf could be given a new lease of life, on sideboards and places of prominence, in homes all over Ireland and beyond, through a bit of artistic ingenuity.

One time, a few years earlier, in an adventurous mood, Willie had undertaken the challenge of carving an entire village from turf. It comprised a number of dwellings, gathered together in the clachan style or arbitrary grouping, which was once commonly found in rural Ireland. An example of a clachan can still be seen in Inishowen, in Ballymagaraghy. There, a cluster of cottages overlook the beautifully situated Tremone Strand, on the northeastern coastline of the peninsula, between Culdaff and Kinnagoe Bay. Willie had constructed a smaller version of the scene, for a relative in 1963. This turf model included a river running under a stone bridge, with dwellings on either bank and a horse drawn cart, with a little man driving it along a narrow road. Every aspect was given attention and the final result was a reconstruction, in miniature, of an important reminder of traditional Irish life, in all the splendour of its unique character.

The later, much larger model was indeed a wonderful achievement. It had required many hours of painstaking work and he had used much effort and skill in the delicate joining together of the individual pieces. His patience was rewarded when the finished article was entered for a competition open to craft workers from all over the county. It won first prize! A prestigious achievement, in the face of strong competition, he had been delighted. His model was featured in the press and was admired greatly by people from near and far. Craft work from the peninsula of Inishowen was on the threshold of being acknowledged throughout the country, due to the high standard that had been set in the village of Culdaff by its native artist.

An occasion, during the previous decade, which had brought even greater pleasure to the painter, who was never one to seek public recognition for his success, was when one of his Donegal Homesteads was presented to the Bishop of Derry at an open air Mass. The scene was at the historic ruin of the church at Cloncha, which is two miles outside his home village. The event was organised by the parishes of Inishowen and a representative from each parish had to make a contribution. The gift chosen from Culdaff was one of Willie's 'wee houses'.

Cloncha was once the site of an important monastery, dating back to the Eighth Century. A large congregation was present when Mass was celebrated beside the remains of the Seventeenth Century plantation church, which stands there today. Willie had felt an enormous sense of privilege when his work was chosen to represent his parish. A keen environmentalist, he had a strong sense of his own nationality, as well as a deeply rooted faith. It was an honour, he considered, that his craft work was chosen, for a number of reasons.

At one level, the subject of the little creations was a modest one. At another level, in their simple and honest portrayal of the essential elements of rural life in Ireland, they embodied a sense of the history which had formed and was continuing to form the people of his land. The tiny dwellings, which he so faithfully represented in all the accuracy of their detail, were reminders of a surviving, indigenous way of life that had developed down through the centuries, from the meagre existence of our ancestors. They were a salute to independence and also to a simplicity of life style which was still being enjoyed by many Irish people, in a world that was slowly being taken over by mass production and the increasing tendency to succumb to excesses in living.

The monastery at Cloncha had been a centre of high artistic achievement. Evidence of this could be found in the richly carved, stone crosses, the remains of which can still be seen in the field surrounding the ruined church. Beautiful manuscripts must have been painted there, Willie often reflected, by pious monks who peered out daily from long, narrow windows, to behold the same hills and plains of a land which had nurtured his own artistic sensibility. It was gratifying that the parish would celebrate an historic occasion with another piece of visual work, derived from its own soil and from the hands and imagination of an artist who was carrying on the same tradition of creative achievement in the area.

A man of simple, regular practice, Willie Doran had great devotion to his religion and was always attentive to the services of his faith. He could regularly be seen on the road leading to the small chapel at Bocan. Often, having already attended morning Mass, he would cycle the mile and a half again, when necessary, for Devotions or a Holy Hour. That usually required having to push the bike a good part of the way, which is nearly all uphill. Time spent in the church was for quiet contemplation of a generous God who had entrusted him with extraordinary gifts. It was also a time to remember his parents and sister Kathleen, as well as many of his old neighbours and friends, who had gone before him to meet that God. With gratitude for being able to serve his community in such a rewarding way, Willie was proud to give his work on behalf of the parish. He was happy to be able to practice within a long tradition of faith and artistic endeavour, in a corner of Inishowen, famous in the past for its monastic and creative achievement. He thanked God frequently that he had been able to live the best part of his life in such a place and that, through his efforts, others had come to share in the rich beauty which he had found within his own surroundings.

Gazing at the three models on the chair in front of him, each at various stages of completion, Willie sighed.

"Work for tomorrow," he thought. Adding that to a large, half finished portrait of a local lady, drawn some days before and now ready for painting, he reminded himself that another two weeks' activities lay waiting to be done.

CHAPTER SIX
Cycling The Peninsula

Guiding the large, black, iron bicycle around the corner and through the doorway of the lower room, it steered out easily onto the street. Although a slight drizzle was threatening to fall from the now heavily laden sky, Willie had decided to risk a quick run to the shore before the three o'clock start in the football field. Dinner had been prepared and eaten. He enjoyed a short cycle in the afternoon and he could not leave it too late, at this time of the year, as daylight would be gone as soon as the match was over. It was almost twenty minutes to two and the dinner dishes, scraped and stacked in the scullery, would have to wait. Feeling a little tired since finishing his meal, he had rested by the fire for a while. The air was colder in the afternoon than it had been in the bright sunshine of the morning. A cycle would warm him up, he thought, before a long stand in the uncompromising and exposed location of the field.

Doran had always been a great lover of football. A familiar figure at all the local matches, he would take up a position near the gate, where he could participate readily in the lively roar of the crowd as they hurled commands of support, or friendly derision, at the young players. A line of cars was usually in attendance, along the narrow car park in front of the pitch. Some observers preferred to view the game from the comfort of a warm seat. Not Willie. He would be out on the field in all weathers, hail, rain and sunshine, revelling in his proximity to the action. In former times he had played football himself. Many of those who now gave their support had also participated in their youth. There was great comradeship in the sport and the Culdaff men used to play, years ago, with teams from Malin village. Malin is four miles away and was considered but a stone's throw of a journey in those days. Cycling was the only mode of transport then for most and huge distances were covered, all around the peninsula and beyond, on bicycles. Willie still cycled daily, using the bike for all journeys within a fifteen mile radius.

In the latter years of the Seventies, there were not too many survivors of the cycling generation. Nowadays cars had taken over and young people no longer considered the bike to be an option. There were still a few stalwarts of the old ways, like himself, who could be seen out on the road, no matter what conditions the weather brought. A number of men continued to make their way to the towns, to the churches, to the pub and to the shop on bicycles. Dark capped figures balanced large boxes of groceries on strong carriers as they returned home, up and down the hills leading from the village. Years of practice ensured that they rarely dismounted, even on the steepest of slopes.

The younger generation preferred to drive, Willie reflected, as he hopped onto the bike and cycled down the hill below his house. The motor traffic had increased greatly in recent years. Soon the cyclist would be a rarity, he thought, making his way through the village, past the Post Office and facing down towards the level road that led to the shore. There would have been throngs of young fellows and girls, twenty years ago, on this road on a good Sunday, heading to the shore on bikes. Summers then saw lanes and roadways lined with streams of energetic cyclists. They would come from as far away as Malin Head, Gleneely, Carrowmore and Glengad, skimming easily over the wide banks of sand dunes, which lie behind the Long Strand. Lifting their bikes up, they would freewheel down easily over the grassy banks, cycling across the golden stretch of sand which runs for nearly a mile along the foaming waves of the Atlantic. Many a romance blossomed in the sand dunes by the shore, as young couples stole away constantly, to escape the curiosity of the crowd. Things were not so sophisticated in those days, Willie thought.

The bike was a luxury when he was young. He remembered the fun of cycling to the pictures in Carndonagh on a Sunday night, years ago. When he was leaving for England in 1948, along with him went his bike. It was necessary then to carry your transport with you on the boat and they were glad to be able to cycle on the other side. The young probably wouldn't dream of it today.

Over the past two months, Willie had undertaken many interesting journeys around favoured parts of the peninsula. Some of these had been for a specific purpose, such as the making of a preliminary sketch for a painting. Others had been taken simply to enjoy the beauty of his native surroundings, in the peace and serenity of a mild autumn climate. He took the roads near Malin and towards Moville, out along the coastline and passing some of the fine scenery which abounds there. Forming part of the stretch of roadway, which encircles the outer perimeters of the peninsula and is known as the *Inishowen 100*, the area contains a generous portion of the most breathtaking landscape to be found anywhere in Ireland.

It was the landscape which had inspired the majority of his own paintings and which, in the intimacy of its small farm dwellings, as well as the awesome vastness of its coastal seas and skies, never ceased to fascinate and intrigue his creative imagination. Every detail caught his attention as he cycled along. He loved the sound of bird call, the feel of the fresh, bracing air and the smell of turf smoke as he passed by houses such as Mickey Logan's, a little thatched cottage at Gortanarin. The cottage is situated some two miles out beyond the Moss Road, between Culdaff and Malin. He had painted the dwelling a few times, once in Spring and also in Autumn. A popular choice of a subject, it catches one's eye on the bend of a corner. Beautifully set among trees, with a distant line of grey blue hills providing a soft, undulating background, the small homestead made a perfect subject.

A particularly enjoyable journey to Malin Head had been taken recently to produce a pencil sketch for the oil painting just completed. Willie had made the trip only a few weeks earlier. Cycling steadfastly, with paints and sketch book firmly clasped on the carrier of his bicycle, he had relished the excursion to the distant location. Arriving at the pier, which nestles in a low, secluded spot, sheltered from the bare, exposed headland which forms Ireland's most northerly outpost, he had picked a suitable vantage point. High above the sea there was a clear view of the complete scene he desired. Beginning to draw, he had noticed the water lapping softly against the pier wall and listened to the seagulls as they flew hungrily, screeching and wailing in their constant search for fish.

Seagulls were something of a trademark in a landscape by Willie Doran. He loved birds and usually included, in his paintings of coastline, a small flock of gulls, dipping and diving over a stretch of sea, or showed two or three picking their way delicately along a wet piece of sand. Each bird would be given a slightly different movement and their broken reflections, mirrored in damp pools of water, were created perfectly using a light touch of the brush. Willie would often stop in the middle of a drawing or painting if his attention was interrupted by the activity of a bird. His sketchbooks featured many tiny studies of creatures which had momentarily caught his eye. He was adept at capturing the fleeting movements of seagulls and crows and always maintained the belief that their inclusion in his paintings created a sense of life within the most desolate of landscapes. The gulls would be a must for this northerly setting, he had noted, as he listened to their plaintive cries in the stillness of the fresh sea air.

On completing the sketch, he had begun the long journey home. Having spent the greater part of the afternoon working, he wished to arrive back before nightfall, so he cycled speedily along the road leading from Malin Head, until he came to the winding corners at Lagg, some few miles outside Malin village. Dusk was approaching as the autumn day hurried to an early close. The reddening sky was magnificent, he remembered, along the coastal road at Lagg where, for a few miles, one can travel in constant view of the broad estuary of Trawbreaga Bay. The high bens of Knocknameny rose up behind him as he sped along. He passed the stark, white shape of the chapel at Lagg, isolated in its situation against the vast, green, undulating dunes that skirt the beach known as the Five Fingers Strand.

Willie had once painted the small, distinctive chapel, from a watercolour produced at this spot. He had also made several drawings of the majestic stretch of shoreline beyond it, a few years earlier. A wild and breathtaking place, the sea there is treacherous. Five short rocks jut out of the water at regular intervals, along the base of the steep, grey cliffs, giving the strand its unusual name. He remembered that he had sketched the scene a number of times before capturing, in a final magnificent pencil study, the essence of a place which has caught the imagination of many artists since. From that drawing an excellent painting in oil had been produced, retaining the vigour which he had witnessed, along a remote shoreline, where waves beat fiercely against the rocky, windswept strand.

Reaching a straight and level part of the road that evening, Willie had slowed down, his eyes almost overwhelmed with the wonderful sight he next beheld. In the stillness of the waning light, a reflection of the Isle of Doagh, across the water from Lagg, could be seen, mirrored perfectly in the calm, full tide. A few white houses were set like precious stones in a purple and green surround and a narrow, golden line of sand at the distant beach shone freshly in the evening glow. No one had passed him on the road as he made his way, cycling ever more slowly, while savouring the breathtaking sight. It was one of those unique experiences, where the unity of colour and stillness can bring a thrill to the senses. How wonderful it was, he thought, that such an experience could be enjoyed only a few miles from home.

One year before, he had stopped a little further along the same stretch of road to capture, in a drawing this time, a similar scene which had taken his attention. It was a harvest field. Darkness had been approaching then also and a flock of rooks had settled there. With hurried strokes, he had sketched the background of the distant hills at Clonmany and the fields near the road, which stretched out before his gaze, hedged in soft, diagonal lines. Without warning, hundreds of birds had risen in a single swoop, the density of their flight almost completely enveloping the sky. Using astute powers of observation, he had reproduced, in a speedily executed pencil study, the effect of the dramatic moment. At home, from memory, he had completed the sketch, filling the vast sky even further with the huge flurry of activity that had been witnessed rising from the darkness of the ground below. This was the drawing that would inspire his painting of birds. It would require courage and daring to recreate the experience of that moment in a large composition, but it would be a challenge for the years ahead and Willie looked forward to it. He had signed and dated the sketch as a reminder of a task still to be done.

A shorter journey, which had brought a great deal of satisfaction to him in recent months, was made in early September to Redford Shore. Taking the coastal road from the village, which leads to the townland of Lecamy and eventually to Moville, one fine sunny afternoon, Willie had travelled to the isolated cove. Redford is a tiny, rocky inlet, which has to be approached by leaving the main road and travelling down a long, narrow and uneven laneway. Off the beaten track, the difficult path requires careful negotiation when pushing a bike. The route back up is a steep incline and also presents a tiring proposition at the end of a day's work. On reaching the shore, however, he had been rewarded by a delightful sight.

A low, grassy headland, nestling against soft, rock strewn sand with a bright, cloudy sky behind and the faint outline of Portaleen beyond, became the inspiration for a lively watercolour. It was an extremely competent work which, in carefully observed hues, displayed Willie's ability to capture the atmosphere of a place with surety, freshness and vitality. He produced it there on the beach, as he sat alone and uninterrupted in the secluded place, sunshine gently warming him, while he laboured over his task. He had signed and dated this work also in the satisfaction that, in his latter years, he could achieve a spontaneous mastery of a technique which he enjoyed using immensely.

The warmth of September suddenly seemed far away that winter afternoon and the memory of his visit to Redford was fading as the chilling bite of December began to take its hold. Pulling his scarf tightly around his neck, Doran brought his mind back to the present, as he pressed his cap firmly down on his head and cycled steadily towards the shore at Culdaff. The rain had stayed, thankfully, at a constant, light drizzle but the air was becoming increasingly cold. Travelling along the shore road was pleasant on a good day and there was usually much to see, although the moist atmosphere of the afternoon caused visibility to be less even. The flat road lies along the river bed, which fills up at high tide and empties when the tide is out, providing a sanctuary for many species of birds. Curlews and herons, among various other types, can be found in the damp habitat, their calls, plaintive and cheery, filling the air night and day.

He passed the tall, stately building of Culdaff House, set elegantly alone among a decorative backdrop of trees and surveying the vast fields which spread out before it. From such an elevated vantage point, the river and the bay, with the harbour beyond at Bunagee, can be viewed easily. He continued to cycle along the gently winding road, which passes by the edge of the fields, forming part of the lengthy estate, until he reached the car park at the shore. Pulling up in front of the Warren Houses, a row of three tall buildings which stand, attached but in isolation there, he dismounted to view the waves. The large, grey dwelling known as Caratra, enclosed behind a high wall and a set of gates, stood silent nearby. It was only inhabited during holiday times then and sat unoccupied, emphasising the solitude of the empty beach.

The ocean stretched out dark and grey, white waves breaking continually against the wet rocks that jutted sharply up from the golden sand. Willie looked across to his right, towards Dunmore Head. How many times had he been asked to paint it, he wondered.

It was his most often requested subject, the feature being synonymous in the popular mind with visitors' memories of Culdaff beach. He had painted Dunmore as a distant headland from across the bay at Bunagee. He had also portrayed it from the intimate viewpoint of Bucker's Rock on the Middle Strand, where attention could be given to a large flurry of waves, breaking against the dark, water stained base of its grass topped, stony form.

Gazing to the left, his eyes rested on the opposite side of the bay where the pier was located, surrounded by the isolated buildings which made up the locality known as Bunagee. Behind the low, grey pier, the familiar forms of Sheep Island and Dun Owen rose up from the rough, foaming water. Heather and gorse covered hillside, which changes dramatically in colour as the seasons pass, made a gentle background for the radiant whiteness of the scattered dwellings and the rectangular, sloping, four-windowed boat house that stood there opposite the pier. A couple of brightly coloured boats sat, tied up for the winter and behind the immediate hills were the steep cliffs which lie in front of the distant headland of Portaleen. The dark, round form of the Cruagh mountain dominated the scene.

Bunagee was one of Willie's favourite places. When he was a very young child, he lived by the old Coastguard Station, before his family moved into the village. The station had ceased to be in use from the early part of the century and for years, following a fire which caused its partial destruction, it remained there as a roofless ruin. Although its site had been filled recently with attractive holiday cottages, Willie still showed the old, derelict station in many of his paintings, feeling that it captured more fully the historic essence of a place he had known and loved.

Having spent some moments feasting his eyes on the churning movements of the Atlantic, he climbed back on his bike to begin the short journey home. The deteriorating weather made the return more difficult. Early drizzle had given way to a constant and severe breeze, carrying with it some spots of icy rain which fell rather ferociously against his face. Cycling on with stoic determination, he passed a few scattered trees along the road, which stretched their dark branches against the heavy clouds.

Willie loved the appearance of winter trees and managed to marvel, in spite of his endeavours to keep warm, at the smooth texture of their silver skins, tautly shining on broad trunks which narrow gracefully into needle sharp twigs. He never ceased to admire trees, as he cycled along at this time of the year, their forms silhouetted against inky hills and the brightly lit skies which herald impending cloudbursts.

Slieve Sneacht stood, mistily veiled behind the village in the distance. The familiar outlines of the church tower, rooftops and clusters of trees seemed further away than usual as he cycled, slowly and carefully, along the empty road. Past the river he went and on until he came to the gate lodge which stands at the entrance leading to Culdaff House. Willie rode past the black gates, glancing briefly towards the dark avenue and then made his way along the narrow lane which links the shore road with the main road to Moville, known locally as the Back Lane. By taking that route he was able to continue the flat, gentle pace of the latter part of his cycle from the shore, rather than return the way he left, which would have involved a short, uphill climb to his home. This way required no extra pushing on the bike. Somehow, he did not feel up to the usual effort that afternoon and looked forward again to a few moments of rest when he would reach the house. Cycling by the Back Lane gave him an opportunity to check if the match was nearly ready to take place. It was and there were even one or two cars parked in front of the field, their occupants anxious to be in position well before the start of play.

Willie cycled on, glad of the level road. He passed Mary Jane Catherwood's cottage, on the corner beyond the field. With its deep, thatched roof, the small house, set now a few steps lower than the road, was the single remaining example of the old style of dwelling left in Culdaff. Glancing at the deteriorating condition of the thatch, he noted with some regret, how so many of the traditional buildings, which he remembered vividly from his youth, were being replaced. It was inevitable, he supposed, that the desire for modern living conditions would soon outweigh the need to preserve such an important part of our heritage, but it was sad to see the old houses falling into decline.

Passing the home of the Lynch family, which stood on the corner a little way past Mary Jane's, Willie's mind wandered back, momentarily, to the years when John worked there as a shoemaker. All around the street a wireless sounded as John Lynch toiled diligently. The smell of leather filled the little workshop while people drifted in and out constantly, with shoes to be mended. The skills of the shoemaker were also on the decline, he feared, as more and more people replaced rather than repaired.

Many important skills had been taught and preserved, down through generations, in that small community. Around the corner his neighbour, Packie O'Connor, had worked for years as a blacksmith, in the forge which gave title to the brae on which Culdaff stood. Packie's father had worked there before him. Willie had often watched horses being led in and out of the busy forge. The sound of iron clanging had been one of those familiar noises with which he had been reared. Large horses, pacing gracefully up and down the road, with their hot breath and widely swinging tails, left an indelible impression in the memory of a child. The services of a blacksmith were no longer needed and the forge had been closed for some years.

Life was changing rapidly in the village. New generations seemed to be adopting a way of life which easily disposed of past knowledge. Instead, many favoured a lifestyle that demanded little in the way of self-discipline and sadly, some showed a less than careful attitude to the needs of the natural environment. Willie perceived this to be a great tragedy, in the latter years of a century which was being hailed for the wonders of its progress.

Leaving thoughts of passing days behind, as he approached the hill where his own house stood, he braked gently to slow himself. Partially dismounting from the bike, he freewheeled down the road and stopped finally on the path outside his home. With an easy turn of the key, the front door opened. The large bicycle was wheeled carefully, through the entrance and back into the lower room, where it would stay till the next journey had to be taken.

25. Evening, Lagg Road
1978
Pencil

26. Willie Doran cycling in Crewe
1950s

27. Lettering a lorry, Crewe
1950s

28. In Culdaff
1970

29. In his kitchen studio, Culdaff
1975

30. Lettering on a van, Crewe (Willie is standing to the left)
1950s

31. Lettering on a delivery van for Daniel Doherty's Bakery, Moville
1973

32. Holding the baby
1960s
Pen and Ink

33. "Have you been waiting long dear?"
1960s
Pen and Ink

34. Mountain Road (detail)
1960s
Emulsion on wall

35. The Pier, Malin Head
1979
Pencil

36. The Five Fingers Strand
1977
Pencil

CHAPTER SEVEN
Fond Reminders

The kitchen was warm and welcoming. Sitting down for a moment to draw his breath, Willie realised that the short cycle had quite exhausted him that afternoon. There was still some time left before the match, so he settled briefly into the chair by the fire for a quick nap. Closing his eyes, he would soon regain lost energy and be ready to enjoy the weekly game with his usual enthusiasm.

The prospect of an afternoon in rain was never enticing at this time of the year and the cold wind had begun to make him doubt if he should venture out again at all. However, he knew that once he had braved the first few moments of a game, he would gradually become so caught up in the excitement of the score, or maybe even the lack of it, weather conditions would not seem so important. There was always plenty of company in the field when a crowd had gathered and he did enjoy the weekly diversion. Looking forward to a bit of excitement from the morning, he would not let the thought of a chilly stand dampen his good intentions. Perhaps he would even complete the night with a quiet drink in Mc Grory's pub.

A couple of drinks in pleasant surroundings was as good a way as any to pass a winter evening in Inishowen. There were four pubs in the village and each had its nightly quota of regular customers. Mc Grory's was the one he frequented as it was only a few steps up the road from where he lived. It provided a pleasant sojourn and he would meet old friends there like Fredrick Lynch, who would take up a stool by the counter, from which he would greet the other patrons as they arrived. The hotel was a bustling entertainment centre during the summer months. In winter it was a quiet place, where a few local customers took their nightly stands at the high counter or sat in clusters around the low, circular tables which were dotted about the comfortable seating area. Men stood along the bar, silhouetted against the bright, yellow glare of the interior, which sparkled warmly with an assortment of bottles and glasses that were displayed on shelves there. Women were few, sitting more often in the carpeted area near the fire, although an occasional female customer braved a tall stool, to enter into the nightly discussions in which men generally had the dominant part.

Willie usually sat on a low seat inside the door, where a row of small stools provided an ideal location for a quiet, uninterrupted evening. He liked to listen to the chat going on at the bar and joined in willingly with an occasional witty remark. Preferring to be a spectator, rather than to be in the centre of things, he was happy to sit back and relax on the fringes of the jovial company. A few hours in the village pub always made a welcome diversion from a long, quiet night in the house. On a winter evening, conversations never varied too much. Usually the weather was a favourite topic. Lengthy discussions were had on the endless changes which take place over the various months of the year. The effects of erratic weather on farming and fishing were often debated, as were political issues north and south of the Border, the proximity of which affected many of the people living in and around Culdaff.

Occasionally the company would be treated to the wonders of the memory capacity of Jim Doherty, known to his neighbours as Jim the Knock. A single man, he lived on a farm a short distance from the village, in an area known as the Knock, hence his name. Jim had the ability to recall a vast number of dates of events which had taken place, locally and world wide, within his own lifetime. He memorised each of these to the exact day and hour. Details of weddings, births and deaths of people throughout the parish, as well as the dates and times of events such as hurricanes and other global disasters, were logged perfectly in his clear memory and could be recalled instantaneously. His talent held the bar-counter audiences spellbound on many occasions. It never ceased to amaze those who listened, how Jim the Knock could have such a wealth of information so compactly stored in his head at one time and how he always had it so readily available on request. An unassuming, courteous and quiet individual, Jim was surely blessed with a photographic memory.

Forthcoming seasons, such as the fast approaching festive time of Christmas, were also discussed enthusiastically at the bar. Married men would lament at the prospect of the annual outlay, while secretly looking forward to the smiles which would await them on their childrens' faces, as an unexpected surprise was received. Willie always looked forward to Christmas. It was a time when he too could become, for a short while, part of family life.

He had celebrated Christmas for many years with the Mc Grorys. On that day he was warmly welcomed into their wide family circle. Arriving at the front door in time for the dinner, he would bring with him the biggest box of chocolates money could buy. The family delighted in his jovial company and John Joe and Deirdre Mc Grory ensured that his day would be spent in a festive and merry atmosphere. He ate turkey and ham, pulled noisy crackers, wore funny hats and watched homemade Christmas pudding being set wonderfully alight in front of young eyes at the dinner table. Willie enjoyed seeing the expression on the childrens' faces when the annual phenomenon took place. He would down large helpings of trifle, which the lady of the house had made potent with generous additions of sherry and all would relax comfortably in front of the television for the afternoon. That was a genuine novelty as Willie did not possess a television set himself.

Sometimes Minnie Doherty, Deirdre's mother, would join them on the day. A retired schoolteacher, Minnie was a lady blessed, like Willie himself, with great wit and the ability to tell a good story. They had passed many pleasant hours, on Christmas Days over the years, telling jokes and stories, discussing politics and a host of other subjects. The more controversial their discussions became, the more they both enjoyed it. The others would feign shock at some of their outrageous comments, but all delighted in the fun that is generated when two good spirits get together. Occasionally, the company would be further enlivened by the presence of Charlie Farren. Charlie had also spent years working in England and would often be at home for Christmas. When Charlie, Minnie and himself gathered together after the dinner, there followed much lively conversation and entertainment. Willie relished those times, marvelling at how the excitement of children and the laughter inspired by good joke telling could bring everyone to life.

A friend of the family for many years, he had worked with the Mc Grorys on various renovating jobs in their premises. James Mc Gonagle, known to all in Culdaff as Wee James, would accompany him during most of the work that was carried out in the hotel over the previous two decades. James was an excellent craftsman and a carpenter by trade. A small, gentle natured man, he and Willie were a delightful combination when working as a team. They toiled hard but joked constantly in mock criticism of each other. Willie was a perfectionist and James, while every bit an expert in his own trade, preferred a less stringent approach. Much teasing and playful scolding took place when they were on a job. They respected each other's abilities, however, and James religiously looked for 'Dorans' approval before ever applying a single spot of paint!

From the time Mc Grory's became a hotel in the mid-Sixties, the local artist's advice and guidance had been sought on their decoration. He chose colour schemes, introduced features such as an authentic wood grain appearance on interior doors and panels and enlivened many walls and corridors with fine mural paintings. As he sat in their pub at night, he could look around and view some excellent examples of his own work. On the wall beside the bar were two landscape murals. These were simple compositions of hills and bog, created using an unusual range of pinks and browns, contrasted with white cottage shapes. They were inspired by the sparse compositions of Achill and Connemara, painted by the artist Paul Henry earlier in the century. The warm hues of the works were surrounded by irregularly shaped, white painted frames, emulating an untreated wood effect. The inclusion of the little compositions generated a soft ambience which blended into the decor of the pub.

Along a narrow corridor outside the bar, Willie had constructed another complex arrangement of drawings. This time, in monochromatic tones, he depicted a variety of scenes, showing different aspects of rural life. Working onto a plain, cream background, he had drawn, in shades of ivory and brown, a series of tableaux. They showed ploughed fields, crows rising from bare trees, a cottage with someone leaning over a half-door and a busy farmyard, with hens running through a wet street towards the dark, distant peaks of a range of hills beyond. Painted frames there also created a three-dimensional effect, suggested using subtle variations of light and shadow. The corridor became, at that time, a virtual gallery, displaying Doran's capability in spontaneous drawing to the full.

A large and colourful scene, produced for an interior section of the bar, was executed on a wooden panel and depicted the bay at Culdaff. Taken from the viewpoint of Dunmore Strand, it showed the landscape seen when looking across towards the harbour at Bunagee. Executed in lively strokes of bold, clear colour, he had suggested the crash of white, foaming waves against pointed, grey rocks and the soft, tonal qualities of sunlight on hills and headlands, as they fade into the distance. A huge array of dramatic clouds completed the tall composition. Willie always enjoyed the freedom afforded in the painting of landscape on this scale. Here, there was no room for fussing and a bold approach suited beautifully his ability to capture the essence of a subject with a few brushstrokes. That mural was designed for distant viewing, as it was originally located in quite an inaccessible place, so a broad approach had been employed. A similar technique had been adopted, some time before, for painting stage scenery in the parish hall at Bocan. Enjoying a worthwhile experience there, working on a backdrop for the stage, he had delighted in the rare opportunity to swap his fine paintbrushes for those of the larger scale used by set designers.

Willie Doran's work in mural painting had become increasingly well-respected over the years. Part of his employment in Crewe had awakened his interest in the painting of interior and exterior murals. He had carried out some large paintings in cinema foyers there and had created huge images on the gable walls of buildings, advertising food products. Skills used for the promotion of products and services in England, were readily adapted for the production of a variety of landscape and figure murals in Ireland. Never one to shirk from a daunting challenge, Willie utilised, continually, the many techniques which he discovered from taking part in all sorts of work, within a range of different practices. His love of experiment was such that he availed of any opportunity to explore new media and approaches. He adapted easily from large scale to small, from two-dimensional to three-dimensional and from commercial subjects to landscape and portraiture. While he had natural preferences, he brought to each facet of his activities a professional standard and was never content to settle for less than the highest quality in any project he undertook. Sometimes there were pieces with which he would express a personal dissatisfaction, but his constant striving to achieve excellence imbued his work consistently with the highest degree of skill and attention.

Alert to ever changing trends in interior decoration, he had created many interesting features in Mc Grory's Hotel over a period of fifteen years. He once mixed a series of unique colour combinations for the painting of architraves and bedroom doors, to tone in with a range of patterns contained in a selection of modern wallpaper designs, which had been chosen by the proprietors. The attention needed to blend the different hues together required painstaking effort, but time was never important to Willie when there were effects he wished to achieve. The result was a beautiful range of subtle colour variations.

While ensuring that the hotel benefitted from his skills as an interior decorator, Willie incorporated his vision as an artist into many of the rooms he designed. To complement the natural wood grain appearance, which he had produced on stairs and doors in the foyer, he invented an interesting focal point for the ceiling. Outlining an abstract shape, he filled it with soft, leafy forms, bringing together a light, harmonious pattern and enlivening the darker effects of the nearby wood. When asked to decorate a panel in one of the bathrooms, a spectacular composition of a ship at sea was created. Tossing in rough, stormy waves, before an evening sky of glowing reds and orange, the subject of the small vessel, struggling against the elements, made exciting viewing for any guest soaking in the large, deep bathtub.

A panel was painted to enliven a space where a door had been replaced in the dining room. The tall, vertical shape of the alcove allowed him an interesting area in which to compose an imaginary rural scene. Willie enjoyed inventing scenes, occasionally, where there was no obligation on him to make reference to known places. He could let his imagination take over and give form to the many lively images that were contained within his head. The result was a bright, fresh picture of summer, painted with ease and providing a welcome focus for guests having a meal in the large dining area.

When a new functions room was opened in 1970, he created a complete range of signs, giving direction throughout the hotel and also produced some fine murals to enhance focal points there. A tall, moonlit scene was undertaken to decorate a vertical corner space. The composition, carried out in muted blues, showed a bright moon reflecting on a calm lake and gave an inspirational feeling to what otherwise may have been an unremarkable corner. The most enduring and impressive image created in the functions room of the hotel, at that time, was a large background panel for the stage. A side panel was also painted, as the stage was set into a triangular shaped corner.

The room was designed to be used nightly, throughout the

summer season, for singsongs, which had increased in popularity over the years. By the time it was renovated, McGrory's singsongs were drawing huge crowds. The proprietors, John Joe and Deirdre, entertained guests with their own singing talents and even brought their young family on stage to perform. Accompanied by Michael Galbraith, an excellent musician from Carndonagh, the Mc Grory couple provided many seasons of entertainment for local and tourist alike.

Those who frequented the musical evenings would often be members of Irish families who had been obliged, in former years, to emigrate. On returning home during the summer, they would naturally enjoy an evening of entertainment in pleasant surroundings. John Joe always provided a good round of suitably heartwarming songs to get the audience into a holiday mood. His songs reflected many of the feelings and emotions experienced by those who had left their native land, as well as reminding all present of the good life to be had then in places like England, Scotland or America, where most of them had settled. Native Scots, English or Americans on holiday in Culdaff and local and returned Irish, all identified with and joined in freely in the lively selection contained within the ensemble.

Having experienced emigration himself, Willie was keenly aware of the importance of enjoying the best of home when on holiday. He wanted to create an appropriate background for the type of entertainment that was being provided in Mc Grory's at that time and painted a scene which could be appreciated by both Irish and tourist audiences. In soft, blue, grey and green shades, he composed a delightful portrayal of a Donegal farmhouse, nestling on the banks of a peaceful lake. Beyond it was a little headland and the high mountain towering behind rose before a gentle sky. Including the small, productive fields of the farm in the foreground, a nostalgic emigrant was treated to a lasting reminder of an Irish smallholding, perhaps not unlike that which he or she had left behind. At the same time, a visitor from abroad could enjoy a scene which was, in every detail, typical of life in rural Donegal. In addition to listening to a feast of song, audiences could experience the delights of the native countryside, when gazing at the beautiful mural. Tastefully coloured, so as not to distract from activities on the stage, the painting provided an atmospheric setting for many outstanding performances which took place in the busy room over the years.

A shorter side panel, although designed to merely complement the larger composition, was actually one of Doran's greatest successes in mural painting. Showing a lightly flowing stream, meandering over a grassed and stony hillside, that painting was carried out with immense speed and dexterity on the part of the artist. It displayed much expertise in the easy portrayal of a difficult subject. Complementary to the more precise detail of the larger panel, the side painting was loosely executed in soft greens and greys. Enclosing the area, it provided another gentle Irish subject on which audiences could feast their eyes.

The young painter, a daughter of the owners, had watched the artist carry out these works in her home. She had stood, enthralled, many times, as he expertly mixed colours, alternating a range of brushes continually, while moving swiftly from large areas to tiny details with a confident touch. She had gazed in admiration as reflections on water and gracefully flying birds had appeared, as if miraculously, under his skilful hand. Willie had given her a box of charcoal when she first expressed an interest in drawing. He had generously primed wooden supports for her early attempts at oil painting. One time, when given the task of including a few cows in a composition, she had been uncertain about where to start.

"There's Willie Doran," her mother had smiled, as he happened to come into the kitchen at just the right moment. "He'll soon show you how to draw a cow." Provided speedily with a piece of old newspaper, Willie had sketched, completely from memory, two perfect cows, grazing along the border of the page.

He advised, but only if requested, giving comments on direction with consideration and tact. Although she still had much to learn, they communicated readily, expressing many similar concerns and sharing a deeply felt joy in the participation of artistic experiences. Seeing her bold attempts had encouraged his search for an expressive emphasis to his work in latter years. He often lamented that he was not achieving that particular goal and recognised that his would always be a traditional approach. He sometimes watched from a distance while she worked. He would pass by on the bike and see her sitting along the shore road, engrossed in a study of landscape. He would notice her behind the bar, sketching portraits of the customers on a quiet night. Sitting discreetly still, as she glanced occasionally in his direction, he was aware that, for a few moments, he too had become a subject. Willie was pleased to see the legacy of painting, which he had practised alone for years in Culdaff, being preserved now in the hands of its young.

Wakening abruptly from his sleep, he rose from the chair. The fire needed attention and would have to be seen to before he left the house. He went to the back door to get some turf from the shed outside and stopped, for a moment, to look vaguely across at the two long gardens, which ran behind his house and O'Connors'. He had often stood there, watching Packie working in his vegetable garden, planting and thinning or raking and gathering, depending on the time of year. Packie O' Connor took a great interest in the garden and supplied his family with a crop of fresh vegetables. Willie grew vegetables himself and had his own supply of potatoes. Self-sufficiency in basic foods such as potatoes, cabbage, scallions or lettuce was taken for granted by a lot of village dwellers at that time and for as long as most could remember. Many hours were spent, by men, toiling diligently in well-developed plots.

Going out into the low shed, he felt for the turf stacked there and lifted a few sods onto his arm. Coming back through the scullery and into the kitchen, Willie checked the fire. It would be adequately stocked now for a while, with the addition of a few new sods. Tiny, red sparks flew merrily into the air, as the weight of the fresh turf caused the already spent pieces to disintegrate wearily, joining a layer of soft ashes at the bottom of the range. Piling the top sods firmly in and pressing the round part of the range top down on them again, he left the remaining fuel in the box beside the stove for later.

His light overcoat, worn earlier for cycling, had been slung over a chair since coming back to the house. Time was slipping by quickly and as it was fast approaching the last few minutes before three, he quickly pulled the same coat on again. Normally, if the weather was as inclement as it had become that afternoon, he would have chosen to wear the heavier overcoat, which was kept hanging in the lower room. The warmth of the kitchen had heated him up surprisingly well and as time was short, he decided he would take his chances with the lighter one. Arranging his scarf to ensure the cold would not affect his neck and throat, Willie put the cap back on his head, pulling it down as far as it would stretch around his ears. He raised his collar and was almost ready to leave.

Darkness was fast approaching as he peered out through the kitchen window, to see if there were any cars on the street. A couple of vehicles drove noisily past. Probably, at that speed, they were on the last minute for a place in the car park in front of the field. Pulling back the curtain slightly, revealed a neat row of sewing needles, stuck into the wallpaper at the side of the window. Long strands of thread hung from them. They were placed there for ease of access, as the tiny instruments served an important purpose. While Willie carried responsibility for most of his own chores, his mending was given to Mollie Mc Colgan, a dressmaker who lived up the road. The needles and thread, at the window, were not for that function.

In addition to the other services which he performed quietly within the community, he was responsible for engraving, on the brass plates of coffins, the names of parishioners who had died. He had carried out this task for a number of years and his fine handwriting skill was requested whenever the occasion arose. The needles held long threads that were used to mark out chalk lines on the plates, prior to lettering. Coating the thread with chalk, it was applied tightly to the surface and pulled to release a thin line of dust, which would act as a guide for the beautiful script he then engraved into the plate.

Willie looked at the patch on the wallpaper, studded over the years with an increasing number of needle points, as they were lifted and returned with what seemed to be a growing regularity. He shook his head and wondered to himself, who would do that job when he was gone?

37. Culdaff Village, Autumn
1977
Pencil

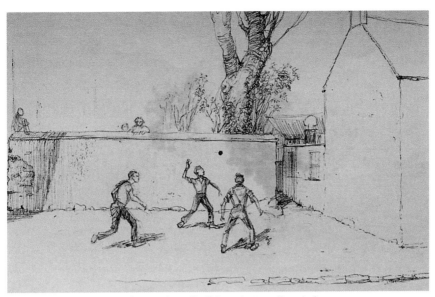

38. Playing handball beside Brodbins' shop
1960s
Pen and Ink

39. Figure studies, playing handball
1960s
Pen and Ink

CHAPTER EIGHT
The Last Match

The short journey seemed to take longer than usual, as Willie Doran made his way steadily over a path that was already well-worn by his own feet. He passed the two large houses beside his home, Devlin's, empty now in winter and Mc Daid's, where a young family eagerly awaited the magical season of Christmas. Arriving at the corner he stopped. He regularly made the same journey, often two or three times a day, for some necessity from the nearby shop. That day being Sunday it was closed. A few steps further around the corner would take him to the football pitch. He could hear noises coming from the direction of the field. A horn blew and shouts of anticipation sounded from the distance, as the players undressed in cars, for their cold, weekly sojourn.

Glancing at the large, plate glass window, which graced the wall of the small grocery shop, he could see the usual assortment of goods displayed there. Household items, non-perishable foods, toiletries and various cleaning utensils were stacked neatly in the wide, open space. Soon it would be decorated for Christmas, Willie thought, as he stood, distracted for a moment, trying to imagine the transformation that would take place over the next few weeks. His journey then would reveal a window, alive with brightly coloured fairy lights and shiny rows of twisted tinsel, to gladden the eye on dark, December evenings.

It was always a delight to behold the shops around the village, dressed in their annual finery. Decorating would take place a week or so before Christmas Day, when an air of excitement seemed to overtake everyone in the locality. Fancy cakes, biscuits and all sorts of chocolates would suddenly appear on shelves. Raisins, sultanas and other delightful ingredients, used in the making of plum pudding and almond iced cakes, were already stocked in abundance, ready for the busy women who were anxious to get their festive baking under way. Toys would be displayed in windows where, for most of the year, a more mundane selection of goods could be found. All the shops in the village carried a quantity of toys and gifts at Christmas, although there was a growing trend lately for people to travel further afield, in search of the wider selection to be found in larger centres like Carndonagh and Derry. The increasing number of families who owned a car, meant that the city and nearby towns were within easier reach and the lure of variety, to be found in large department stores, presented a growing enticement.

Willie remembered a time when people wouldn't have dreamed of leaving their own locality to shop. Culdaff once supplied the surrounding area with all its needs. When he had returned to the village in 1962, it had boasted no less than nine shops and these had even increased to ten as the decade progressed. However, the Seventies, now drawing to a close, had witnessed great changes in the retail trade. Decimalization and the introduction of the supermarket had given rise to a completely new approach to shopping, from that which people of his generation had known.

At one time, the village store was one of the principal meeting places in the parish. People gathered to buy goods, but also to exchange views and to pass comment on items of news in the area, as well as in the world at large. A shopkeeper had to be host, servant and cheery mediator of arguments, in addition to being extremely nimble of mind and body. The variety of products available in an outlet then, meant that a single customer's visit could have an assistant running steadily, from one activity to another, for a good fifteen minutes or more.

Shopkeepers didn't have it easy in those days, Willie reflected, as he dallied momentarily at the corner. The purchase of something like bacon involved the manipulation of huge rolls, which hung from hooks in the back of a shop. These had to be carefully negotiated off the wall and cut to a manageable size, ready for the sharp bacon slicer. Bags of flake meal or Indian meal were filled by the scoop, from large sacks which were kept in store houses outside. Heavy scales were used for their measurement and the shopkeeper's accuracy was of the utmost consequence. Snuff was delicately spooned into tiny bags, from a strong smelling, tightly sealed box on the counter. Plug tobacco had to be gauged by the eye, cut and weighed. Biscuits were stored in glass-fronted, tin boxes and measured out on request into paper bags, assortments often being left to the discretion of an assistant. Bread was unsliced and had to be wrapped in brown paper. In the heat of a summer's day, the request would arise for a thick wafer of ice cream to be cut and woe betide anyone who sold a customer short on the size of a wafer! Paraffin oil had to be filled into bottles and metal containers from huge tanks, usually situated at draughty and exposed sites in a yard outside the building. It was not a pleasant job on a winter's evening.

Prepackaging of goods had increased in recent years, relieving greatly the work of the shop assistant, but some of the old routines were still followed. Attendants had to be experts in arithmetic, as prices were calculated on paper when orders were complete. Tall sums were totalled on the spot and a pleasant countenance maintained, while a queue of customers stood waiting to be served. Mathematical accuracy and good humour must have to be two of the most important qualities in an efficient shopkeeper, Willie often thought.

As he stood looking into the dark window, he reflected briefly on how much a part of the life of the village the small stores had played, down through the years. There were the deliveries to the various destinations. Bread vans, fruit wholesalers and lorries bringing a variety of other products, were a familiar sight on the street, early in the mornings and on some afternoons during the week. Greeting all with their well-seasoned and cheery banter, the deliverymen always produced a welcome and lively diversion within a street, silent in winter, for a few hours daily, without children. Some of the vans, that passed by his home, displayed signs which Willie himself had painted, his expertise bringing tastefully constructed advertising to enhance an awareness of their products, as they travelled throughout the peninsula.

The shops served a wide community. Pension payments on Fridays took car and vanloads of elderly people to Culdaff. Many of them, from outlying areas of the parish, brought with them their own peculiar brand of humour. The village would fill for an hour, once a week, with their lively chat. Anecdotes and sharp remarks, levied good naturedly at each other, was the order of the day and the weekly outing was an opportunity to rekindle old neighbourly rapport. Transported first to the Post Office for pension collection, a convenient store then offered a place where some essential items could be purchased. There, in the presence of a good-natured assistant and old comrades from past days, many relived the fun and companionship that was once a part of their lives, at a time when they were more active and independent. For those members of the community, it was an essential meeting place and the friendly interaction was a significant part of their weekly routine.

Younger women were the most frequent customers in the village, but men were regularly sent when there was a long list. Boxes, loaded with groceries and bound with string, were carried home weekly, on bicycle carriers, tractors and more often recently, in cars. Some people, like himself, acquired daily supplies, the familiarity of their surroundings enabling all to make easy recollection of their needs.

Willie always enjoyed creating a bit of fun when he called in for a message. Being a natural comedian, he managed to introduce an element of lightheartedness into the purchase of any item. In years gone by, when he used to smoke, his request for a packet of ten Carroll's Number One cigarettes and a box of matches became "Ten wans and a match o' boxes."

He constantly turned words back to front for a laugh and never missed an opportunity to create a comical statement out of the simplest of sentences. Whistling jovially as he entered the shop, he would ask for his habitual "wee tin o' beans" or a "wee shape for the tea". A shape was a long, narrow loaf, suited to the requirements of a single man. A sunny day would find him arriving up briskly for "a wee packet o' Surf for the clothes." Pulling funny faces was part of his routine, greatly exploited over the years by a fascinating ability to move his mouth in a number of hilarious positions. Although a private person in most aspects of his personality, Willie was also a born performer who, among friends, enjoyed the thrill of making people laugh. His cheery introductions brought a regular spark of humour into the long day of many a tired assistant, who had spent time tending to the needs of other more demanding and much less entertaining customers.

A trip to the shop provided him with a welcome break in the middle of a painting or other complicated piece of work. Living alone and working in his home, it was an environment where, on stepping through the door, one was instantly guaranteed company and conversation, as well as the simple supply of goods for daily living. One of the village shops had actually been an excellent subject for painting. Brodbins', which was visible from Dorans' kitchen window, was painted by him a number of times. Now closed since the death of its proprietor, Joe Brodbin, the picturesque building had given Willie much inspiration throughout the last seventeen years.

In sunshine, an awning over its two large, square windows shaded an assortment of goods displayed there, with jewellery and drapery at one side and groceries on the other. In its heyday, the faint tinkle of a bell over the door could be heard around the street when a customer entered or left. Pink marbled cakes were prominently set out on a wooden counter, beside colourful arrangements of sweets and other edibles, while a glass topped case housed a selection of exotic goods, ranging from round, plastic earrings to Irish souvenirs. A tall, stately building, dating back to the early part of the century, it had three pointed windows in a steep, grey slated roof and stood quaint in its setting at the bottom of the green. Brodbins' made extremely interesting viewing, Willie had always felt.

Sadly, some of the retail services that had been such a part of village life, now no longer existed. This had happened partly due to the demise of their owners, with no one to replace their skills, as well as being a reflection of the growing change in trends. There was once a butcher in Culdaff. Other outlets had provided, within their premises, drinking facilities. General supplies could be purchased at one counter and a bottle of stout at the other. Items like clothes and shoes, that had been sold in the village at one time, were no longer sought, due to the increasing availability of transport and a greater selection in the larger towns.

Most of the shops that remained now carried only a limited supply of grocery and household requirements, although they managed to retain their unique specializations. One dealt in toys and items of interest for children. Another sold hardware and fishing tackle. Seasonal goods were stocked by all, to accommodate tourists in the summer. Each had its loyal clients, depending on proximity to outlying areas or the preferences of individuals. There was plenty of variety once in the village and some of it was still in existence, Willie thought thankfully, as he lingered for a moment longer at the familiar corner.

However, the ten busy stores of the early days had dwindled to seven. The practice of travelling to seek value elsewhere was probably going to continue. In time, the village would not sustain the vast changes which were taking place, he feared, as he considered the impact that had been brought about over just a few years. No doubt, in the future, some of the remaining shops would also have to close. It would be a great loss to the local people, he considered, if that aspect of life were to fade away completely. Large supermarkets would probably provide a broader range of goods and possibly more value for money, but they could never replace the sense of community that was to be found in a small shop. For people like himself, the existence of the family run business gave regular hospitality and a sense of homeliness to their customers, as well as providing a necessary service. Without such a facility, Willie realised, as he walked on towards the field, life would be a very isolated existence.

A crowd had gathered at the football pitch. Cars were lined up along the park and some of the players were out on the field. Walking the last hundred yards more speedily and with a growing sense of purpose, he joined a few men who were waiting for the game to start. He pulled his collar more tightly about him as the December chill continued to maintain an icy grip. Realising by now that the warmer coat would definitely have been a better option, Willie wondered if he should return immediately to the house and make a change. The match was beginning and a decision would have to be postponed, he decided, trying vainly to convince himself that he would become acclimatised to the increasingly harsh conditions, as the game wore on.

The air was bitter as serious play began. Staunch supporters marvelled at the perseverance of the young players who hopped constantly from one leg to the other, rubbing their hands together viciously in an effort to keep warm. Later, the rush of adrenaline that is created when the tension of a game takes over, would ensure for them at least, a temporary reprieve. Lively comment passed the time during the cold stand of the first half. Hot whiskeys were anticipated by a few supporters, who had faithfully braved the severe conditions, to give active encouragement along the side. Men joked about the folly of their purpose, out in the unrelenting weather when they could have been sitting at home in front of a well stocked fire. Willie nodded, smiling in agreement as he stood quietly, his hands thrust deeper and deeper into the pockets of his coat, unable finally to escape the cold feeling of unease which was beginning to cause him some discomfort, as the minutes went by. Eventually the whistle would blow to mark the arrival of half time. Grasping an opportunity, he decided to make the journey back home to fetch his warmer coat.

A cloud had descended over the top of Slieve Sneacht, which could be seen in the distance from the field, as Doran left the crowd. He walked the brief journey back around the corner, his head bent in an attempt to shield his face from the severity of the wind. The wet, grey sky, that had been so bright and encouraging in the morning, now contained all the signs of a damp and blustery evening. Soon it would be so heavily laden, night would surely come quickly.

Opening the front door, he felt the familiar rush of heat emanating from the stove in the kitchen. It filled the house with a warm and welcome glow. He stepped into the lower room, which was shadowy now in the quickly fading light. Without turning on the switch, he reached towards the low hook where his heavy coat hung. Removing the lighter one slowly, he allowed its weight to slip comfortably over his shoulders, bringing to his now aching bones, a final sense of well-being. Buttoning the coat to maintain his newly found warmth, Willie opened the door of the kitchen to check the fire.

It seemed to be in order and he was thankful that there was sufficient fuel left to save him from having to go back outside again, later in the evening. He had switched on the light and the brightness of the yellow bulb bathed the small area with a soft radiance. The kettle on the black range sat full and partially heated. Within minutes it could be gently steaming on the range top, invitingly suggesting now that he partake of the sustenance of a hot cup of tea. It was a tempting thought and Willie hesitated, arguing with himself about the wisdom or folly of the suggestion. Finally he resisted, knowing that the time was not long enough to dally over what increasingly seemed to be an act of supreme luxury. He turned slightly and was ready to leave the house.

Unexpectedly, he thought of his mother, sitting by the fire with the melodeon on her knee. In his mind's eye and with a startling clarity, he visualised the young family that once sat around her, with his father looking on. For a few timeless seconds, it seemed as if the silent kitchen had filled again with their noisy laughter and the sweet sounds of old, forgotten tunes. It was a joyful experience and Willie found himself wishing that the happy recollection would last forever, particularly on a day which had already been filled for him with many fond reminders. He blinked his eyes, trying to hold on to a scene that faded softly into the distant corners of his mind, to be replaced once more by the quiet contents of the empty room and the sound of a clock gently ticking. Only on the walls did his paintings continue to give singular approval to a life filled with much satisfaction, in spite of the absence of those whom he loved. As he gazed around the room, the pictures that hung there seemed to shine and glow, in the momentary presence of the people who had first nurtured the development of his gifts.

Doran had to drag himself forcibly back to the reality of his purpose. A faithful supporter, he persuaded himself at last to return for the rest of the match. Glad of the relative comfort being provided by the change of overcoat, he reached towards the light switch and left the kitchen in darkness.

There were few on the street as he walked back towards the field. A passerby enquired as to the reason why he had rushed off in the middle of a game.

"The old coat was too light," came the short reply, as he hurried back to the sounds of the first half, nearly over. A warm memory of his own people filled his head as Willie approached the field, thanking God silently for the beautiful moment he had just experienced. He took up the same spot which he had left earlier and where he had stood, through many years of watching football, near the gate at the main entrance to the field. The players were stopping the action as he arrived and everyone was beginning to wind down for a well deserved break. Poor weather conditions had not abated and the chill in the air was unrelenting. Fixing his eyes on the activity, he attempted to discern the state of play.

The home team had been fighting against the wind and Doran offered a few words of encouragement as they made their way out of the gate.

"You'll get them in the second half," he called to David Mc Laughlin, the last of the players to leave, as they ran towards the temporary shelter of the cars.

David smiled and had no sooner passed when suddenly and without warning, Willie stumbled and fell to the ground. The young players who had reached the car park, raced back immediately, but they could see he was not moving.

"Willie Doran has collapsed!" someone shouted, as people ran from the side of the field towards the spot where he had been standing, chatting, only moments earlier. They stopped, shocked and speechless when they found him lying motionless, on the grass. Within seconds everyone knew that something terrible had happened.

Carefully, three men lifted him and carried him across the road to Mc Grory's. A dark sky enshrouded the December afternoon, as they made their sorrowful journey, hoping, in a desperate bid, to be of some assistance. It was too late. A glass of brandy had been hastily poured, in an effort to bring revival. It was never used. Although two local nurses and the doctor were quickly on the scene, attempts at resuscitation were in vain. Willie had suffered a heart attack and death had come instantly. Neighbours stood by in disbelief, not knowing what to say or do. How could it have happened so quickly? Wasn't he talking to someone a few minutes earlier? Sure he was enjoying the football as much he ever did on a Sunday? Didn't he pass us on the bike this morning going to Mass?

Gradually the truth began to dawn. Willie Doran was dead. The humble artist, who had shared their lives, for as long as many there could remember and who could enliven any gathering with his ready wit, was gone. He had left them quickly and unexpectedly. It was sad, people remarked afterwards, that he had died while watching a football match. Yet, many acknowledged also that there could not have been a more appropriate place. Willie was happy when he was engaged in the activities that he loved and after painting, football was his favourite passion. Ironically, one of his last commissions had been to paint the famous Irish rugby captain, Tom Grace, in action. Working from a photograph which had appeared in a national newspaper, Doran had recreated a dynamic image of a vigorous athlete in full flight. Against the colourful background of Landsdowne Road, with a crowd cheering and the Irish flag flying, he had paid personal tribute to a sporting hero.

That Willie should end his life against a similar, if more modest backdrop, may not have been entirely displeasing to him. Among his own people, in a place that he cherished, doing something he enjoyed? He probably wouldn't have had it any other way.

EPILOGUE

Willie Doran was laid to rest in the family grave, inside the gates of St Mary's Church at Bocan, following his death on the 2nd of December 1979.

The young artist visited his house a few days later. There, in the lower room, was the painting of Malin Head. She had not returned in time that Sunday afternoon and when she beheld the beauty of his final composition, she realised why he had asked her to view it. Here was a painting that had everything associated with the best of Willie Doran. The sea was a radiant blue and the sky showed a sense of promise, in the soft, rain tinged clouds that floated nonchalantly over the distant horizon. Seagulls flew merrily, as if unaware that anything tragic had happened. It was a fitting conclusion to his life's work, she thought.

For many mornings to come, she would pass his window, silent without the comfort of his smiling presence. Often, in the years that followed, she would stop and press her face against the small panes, peering into the empty kitchen where familiar pieces of furniture sat idle since his death. For a long time the house lay empty, yellow chairs and painted fireplace still visible through the glass. Eventually it was demolished and a new building constructed in its place.

The treasured pictures had been removed, following the artist's death and found homes with family and friends. There they continue to hold pride of place and will be admired and enjoyed for many years to come. A number of Willie's fine murals shared the fate of his house, succumbing to the perils of damp and age.

Some were destroyed during the process of renovation but others have been preserved and still bear witness to the talent of their creator. As most of his work was produced on commission, paintings can be found throughout Ireland and in England, Scotland and America. All are in private collections.

A posthumous exhibition, of the work of Willie Doran, was eventually held in 1990 in Culdaff, to mark the launch of the Charles Macklin Autumn School. The annual festival, which is organised by members of the local community, celebrates the accomplishments of another native of the area, the great Shakespearean actor and playwright, Charles Macklin, who was born in Gortanarin in the Seventeenth Century. It was an opportunity for people to see many fine examples of work by the Culdaff artist and to experience, perhaps for the first time, the range of his talent. For many years, a memorial football league celebrated Willie's dedication to the game. It was hosted by the village under the title The Willie Doran Cup.

Some people live and work so quietly and humbly that their passing often goes unnoticed. Others make such an impression on those who knew them, that their memory is carried on successfully from one generation to the next. Willie combined both of these qualities. At the time of his death, Brian Bonner accurately described him as being gentle, unobtrusive and self-effacing.

He never sought publicity but was an active member of the local community, working steadfastly, in a quiet and personal way, towards fostering a respect for the environment in which he felt very privileged to live and work. A modest existence was probably the key to his contentment. He accepted the opportunities that arose in his lifetime and experienced each to the full. He lived simply and died peacefully. Throughout his career, Willie Doran touched many people with his mastery of skill and the power of his perception. In the surroundings of his native Inishowen, he expressed fully the range of his creative capability.

He taught by example rather than by words. His lifestyle and dedication to his craft was an inspiration for any young person, aspiring to the rewarding but difficult career of an artist. Perhaps the greatest tribute to the painter from Culdaff is that words are never necessary to describe the work of his hand. Its excellence could and always will speak for itself.

40. The Winner !
1960s
Pen and Ink

ON THE PAINTING OF MALIN HEAD
In memory of Willie Doran

As a gull spreads its wings on a cloud-building sky
And a wave, white and brittle with rain,
Lights a path in my mind to some few days gone by,
I can feel how you looked on the same.

As the Inishowen isles raise their heads from the sea
And the sand is washed golden with foam;
Many joyful impressions come racing to me
Of a voice that grew sure but unknown.

Of a hand that grew freer with every new day
And an eye that was practised and true;
Of a magical power to express and to say
A delight in a vision that's new.

Yes, we talked and discussed in the seldom spared times.
Did I utter a critical word
When you'd ask an opinion of a doubt in your mind?
If I did, now in sorrow I'm heard.

For you listened with interest when I spoke my raw praise
And as only true Masters can do,
You expressed a delight in my clumsy new ways.
I cared about failing on you.

From my own short encounter I've learned something great,
Which I've not realised till you've gone;
That the praise and the glory in this life can wait
But it's only the soul that lives on.

And it's only someone with a dream that is clear
Who can speak out that dream constantly,
For no words can translate what is private and dear.
Thoughts don't suffice for what's to say.

They gave me your brushes and the tools that you used
And I humbly accepted them all,
Though they never will wield that great power and life
And those fine strokes will not again fall.

But I'll stand on the shore and I'll look at the waves
And I'll learn about colour and light.
In my own awkward way I will carry your flame
Of a simple love for what is right.

And some day, there maybe just will come a time
When I'll ask someone who is young
To observe my last work, in the peak of my prime,
And he also may cry, as I've done,

When he looks at a sea that is dipped in a pool
Of the colours God's own eye has made;
When he sees the soft haze of a sky that is full
Of a promise of sun, that has strayed.

Perhaps this expectation is life's dream fulfilled.
Surely this is the dream that's sublime.
Then you've earned your reward for the work that you've done
And the genius we knew is divine.

Deirdre McGrory (Devine)
December 1979

BIBLIOGRAPHY

Arnold, Bruce	Mainie Jellett and The Modern Movement in Ireland
Bonner, Brian	Our Inishowen Heritage
Cahill and Company	Irish Art Handbook Published in Dublin 1943
Egan, Patrick K	St Brendan's Cathedral, Loughrea, Co. Galway The Irish Heritage Series: 56
Gordon Bowe, Nicola, Caron, David, Wynne, Michael	Gazeteer of Irish Stained Glass
Gordon Bowe, Nicola	The Life and Work of Harry Clarke
Harrison, Graham	Saint Eunan's Cathedral, Letterkenny, Co. Donegal The Irish Heritage Series: 62
Mc Grory, Neil	Inishowen - A Journey through its Past
O'Grady, John	The Life and Work of Sarah Purser
Wynne, Michael	Irish Stained Glass The Irish Heritage Series:1
The Artist Vols. 35 - 49	Published by The Artist Publishing Co. Ltd. 33 Warwick Square, London
Derry Journal Jan.11 1980	Culdaff Artist's Death An appreciation by Inishowen Historian Brian Bonner
Irish Arts Review 1994	An Túr Gloine Stained Glass in Arizona by David Caron